TIME

THOMAS

EDISON

TIME

Thomas Edison

His Electrifying Life

Editor / Writer Richard Lacayo
Designer Arthur Hochstein
Photo Editor Patricia Cadley
Reporters Jenisha Watts, Mary Hart
Copy Editor Jane Sandiford
Editorial Production David Sloan, Lionel Vargas

Time Home Entertainment
Publisher Jim Childs
Vice President, Business Development and Strategy Steven Sandonato
Executive Director, Marketing Services Carol Pittard
Executive Director, Retail and Special Sales Tom Mifsud
Executive Publishing Director Joy Butts
Director, Bookazine Development and Marketing Laura Adam
Finance Director Glenn Buonocore
Associate Publishing Director Megan Pearlman
Assistant General Counsel Helen Wan
Assistant Director Special Sales Ilene Schreider
Book Production Manager Suzanne Janso
Design and Prepress Manager Anne-Michelle Gallero
Brand Manager Michela Wilde
Associate Prepress Manager Alex Voznesenskiy
Associate Brand Manager Isata Yansaneh

Editorial Director Stephen Koepp
Editorial Operations Director Michael Q. Bullerdick

Special Thanks to:
Katherine Barnet, Jeremy Biloon, Susan Chodakiewicz, Rose Cirrincione, Lauren Hall Clark, Jacqueline Fitzgerald, Christine Font, Jenna Goldberg, Ricardo Santiago, Hillary Hirsch, David Kahn, Amy Mangus, Robert Marasco, Kimberly Marshall, Amy Migliaccio, Nina Mistry, Dave Rozzelle, Adriana Tierno, Vanessa Wu, TIME Imaging

Published by TIME Books, an imprint of Time Home Entertainment Inc.
135 West 50th Street • New York, NY 10020

ISBN 10: 1-61893-057-5
ISBN 13: 978-1-61893-057-6
Library of Congress Control Number: 2012955016

We welcome your comments and suggestions about TIME Books. Please write to us at:
TIME Books, Attention: Book Editors, P.O. Box 11016, Des Moines, IA 50336-1016.

Some material in this book appeared previously in TIME or on Time.com

Edison speaks into the recording tube of a graphophone, a dictation device based on the phonograph.

CONTENTS

The usually inexhaustible Edison, who often worked late into the night, grabs a catnap at his West Orange lab.

THE MAN WHO INVENTED OUR WORLD

INTRODUCTION By Richard Lacayo

How much did Americans revere Thomas Edison in his lifetime? Enough so that when one of New York's largest newspapers, William Randolph Hearst's *Journal*, decided in 1897 to serialize a science fiction novel, it was something called *Edison's Conquest of Mars*. Millions of readers thrilled to the story of Martian invaders being chased back into space and defeated on their home planet by Earthlings under Edison's leadership. To ensure victory, the suavely brilliant inventor produces an antigravity flying machine and a "disintegrator" gun that he demonstrates for his comrades by zapping a crow. When the hapless bird instantly dematerializes, the Terminator of Menlo Park says coolly, "That looks bad for the Martians, doesn't it?"

MAKING SOUND COME ALIVE

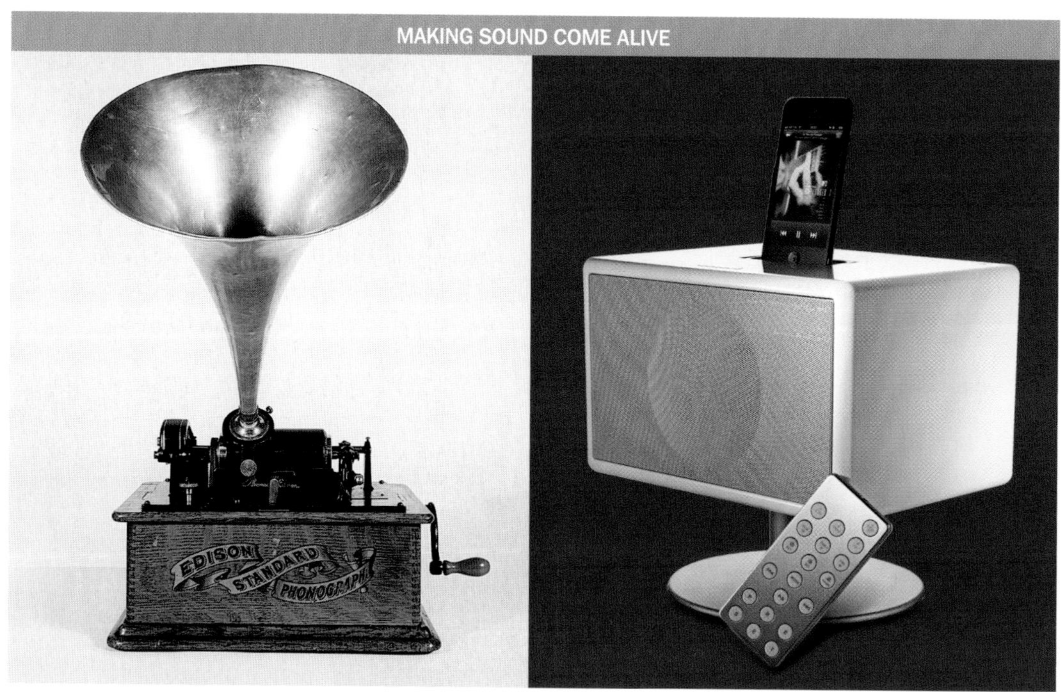

From Edison's lab came innovations that laid the groundwork for the technology-driven world we live in today.

Of course a world under attack from an advanced civilization would turn to Edison as its savior. From his early 30s, he was the very embodiment of the genius inventor, the man whose laboratories poured forth devices that defined the modern world. First came the phonograph, a machine that miraculously recorded and preserved voices and music, and more miraculous still, played them back again. Everything from the hi-fi to the iPod followed. Later he would produce a gadget that preserved movement, the movie camera, the little box that launched the big industry called filmmaking. But above all, there was the light bulb, or at least the first practical incandescent bulb, as well as the system of generators, wires, and switches to power it and all the other electrical ma-

LIGHTING UP OUR LIVES

chines and appliances Edison's mastery of electricity made possible.

We take electricity so much for granted now that it's hard to appreciate how profoundly it changed the day-to-day experience of life. Or rather, night to night. Although candles, oil lamps, and gaslight had preceded it, the electric bulb truly brought nighttime into the light and made it an active part of each 24-hour cycle. Sundown no longer marked the moment when the world got ready for bed. In 1929, speaking at a grand celebration of the 50th anniversary of electric light organized by Henry Ford to honor his dear friend Edison, President Herbert Hoover tried to summarize the many ways electric light had changed life for the better:

> *It enables our towns and cities to clothe themselves in gaiety by night, no matter how sad their appearance may be by day. And by all its multiple uses it has lengthened the hours of our active lives, decreased our fears, replaced the dark with good cheer, increased our safety, decreased our toil, and enabled us to read the type in the telephone book.*

Some of his listeners might very well have been aware that electricity had also made possible a world of garish electric signs and round-the-clock working hours. But even they would probably have agreed that, on balance, electric light and power had been one of the great gifts to civilization. And that gift had come largely from Edison. Notwithstanding that over the years many scientists and inventors had contributed to developing the bulb, that much of the work in Edison's lab was done by his assistants, and that by 1929 the world was actually operating on the alternating current promoted by his competitors, the essential insights in the realm of electric light and power came from Edison, and also no small part of the long hours of labor. The man who said that genius was "one percent inspiration and ninety-nine percent perspiration" had his own sweat in mind.

About those laboratories. What makes Edison not just a hero of innovation but also a very modern kind of inventor is that he pioneered the industrial research and development laboratory.

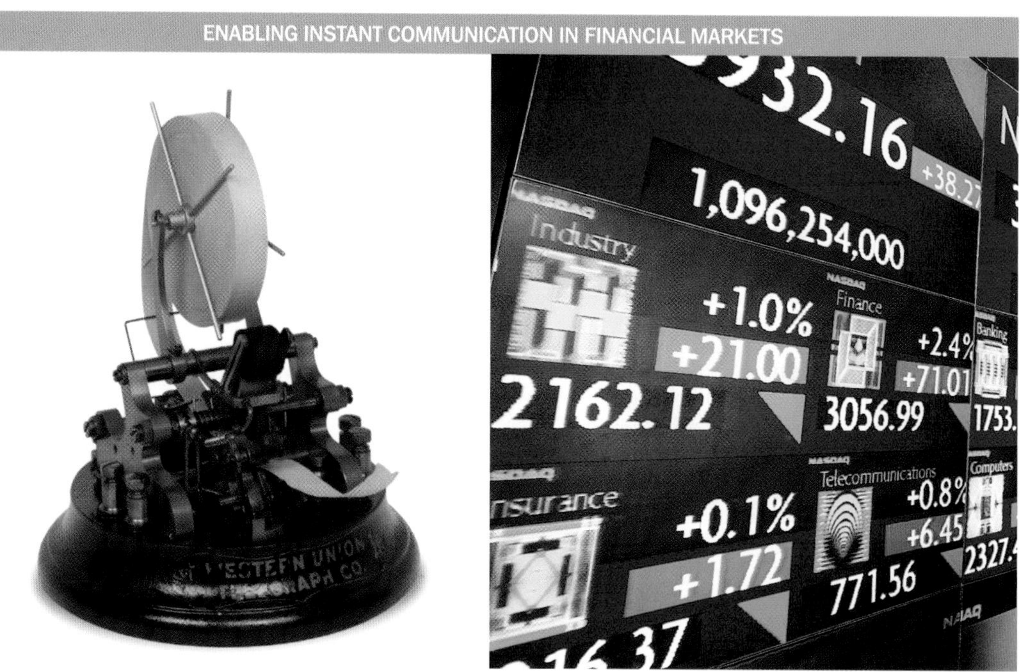

ENABLING INSTANT COMMUNICATION IN FINANCIAL MARKETS

The 19th century thought of inventors as lone wolves, solitary men of applied science who arrived at their new machines with one or two assistants at most. Until Edison, that picture was more or less accurate. But his facilities at Menlo Park and then West Orange, N.J. , and the large teams of research assistants he assembled to work with him, were the precursors of the vast R&D operations we now associate with Bell, Microsoft, Apple, and Google.

Yet what made Edison so well suited to the role of America's favorite inventor was not just his purchase on the future but also his comforting aura of the past. He had a homespun quality that made him the ideal man to point a mostly rural nation into a new world of ceaselessly changing technologies. He came from a family of modest means, was raised in small towns in Ohio and Michigan, had almost no formal schooling, and though he became a wealthy man, never entirely seemed like one. What he seemed like was a blunt-speaking American with dust on the lapels of his jacket.

And very much that favorite American archetype, the self-made man. Henry Ford is supposed to have called Edison "the world's greatest inventor and world's worst businessman" because of how often Edison blundered in the attempt to make money from his revolutionary creations. But if he had more than his share of business setbacks, most of them self-inflicted, it did not go unnoticed that he constantly picked himself back and up and tried something new. In the late 1880s, Edison was visited by Henry Stanley, the journalist/explorer who had tracked down Dr. Livingstone. After Edison demonstrated his phonograph for him, Stanley asked what voice from the past he would most like to hear. "Napoleon's," Edison said. Stanley replied that he wanted most to hear "the voice of our savior."

"Oh well," Edison shot back. "You know, I like a hustler."

So he was a man with all the right qualities to change the world—brains, energy, and daring. Just the fellow you would want to lead you into battle against the Martians. No wonder his fame has lasted. If you're reading this book by the light of an incandescent bulb, you might even say Edison is looking over your shoulder still. Tell him "thank you" before you turn it off.

BIRTH OF AN INVENTOR

CHAPTER ONE

Thomas Edison, a man who would do so much to change the world, came into the world at what was already a transitional moment in American life. He was born on Feb. 11, 1847, in Milan, Ohio, then a fast-growing town on the Huron River, eight miles from Lake Erie. James K. Polk was president. The country was in the midst of the Mexican-American War, as well as an escalating struggle over slavery. It was also on the threshold of an industrial transformation. In northern states, small manufacturing was flourishing in industries such as textiles, firearms, and furniture. Cyrus McCormick was perfecting the mechanical reaper, and Elias Howe the sewing machine. Canals were spreading everywhere, and a decades-long railway boom would soon be under way. But America was still largely a rural nation, even in the more industrialized North. The census of 1850 counted almost 23.2 million people, more than half of them living on farms.

Thomas Alva Edison at age 14. Those who remembered him in his childhood—when he was known simply as "Al"—recalled that he was full of curiosity about the world.

The year of Edison's birth was also a time of rudimentary medicine and high childhood mortality, as his own family history testified. He was the last of seven children, but three died before he arrived, one at the age of six and two others in infancy. Because his three surviving siblings were already in their teens when he was born, they were soon out of the house. Edison was essentially raised as an only child, which may have contributed to his lifelong taste for solitary work and study.

Although his forebears had long roots in the U.S., this celebrated American inventor came close to being born a Canadian like his father. His great-grandfather, John Edison, the first of the American line of the family, had arrived in New Jersey in the early 18th century, probably from the Netherlands. But throughout the Revolutionary War, John and his wife, Sarah, remained fiercely loyal to the British Crown. After the war, they were expelled with other loyalists to Canada, settling first in a bleak forested tract of Nova Scotia. After 28 years of struggle, they moved to gentler territory in Ontario, just north of Lake Erie.

Though Edison's father, Samuel Ogden Edison Jr., was the grandson of these staunch Tories, he would grow up to oppose British rule in Canada. In 1837, when Sam was a 33-year-old tavern keeper and political firebrand, he took part in a short-lived armed rebellion against the royal government of Canada. When the uprising failed, he fled on foot to the U.S., temporarily leaving behind his American-born wife, the former Nancy Elliott, and their four children.

Fetching up in Milan, Sam Edison soon managed to re-establish himself in business, starting a mill that cut wood shingles. He rightly anticipated that a new canal connecting Milan to a navigable part of the Huron River, and from there to Lake Erie, would make the town a thriving port and set off a building boom. Within two years he felt secure enough to summon his family to join him. In preparation for their arrival he purchased a one-acre lot and built the brick house where his first and last American-born child, Thomas Alva Edison, would eventually come into the world.

The boy took his first name, Thomas, from Sam's brother. Alva was a tribute to Alva Bradley, an American barge captain who had lent Sam money to help him start his shingle mill. As a boy, the young Edison was known to most people as "Al." In later years, people who knew him in childhood remembered his curiosity about the world around him. When he was just six, he was so anxious to discover what would happen if he set a fire in the family barn that he burned it to the ground, prompting his father to subject him to a public whipping with a wooden switch in the town square.

By then, the Edison family fortunes had begun to take a turn for the worse. After a rail line was completed between Norwalk and Toledo, Ohio—bypassing Milan and making its canal less important as a shipping route—the once booming town went into a swift decline. Sam Edison's mill business declined with it. In search of new opportunities, in 1854 he moved with his wife and seven-year-old son to Port Huron, Mich. Even in their reduced circumstances, the Edisons managed to obtain a spacious house; but they were renters this time, not owners. And they would never again be truly prosperous. In the coming years, Sam would try his hand at the lumber, grain, and feed businesses, without much success.

It was in Port Huron, in the autumn of 1855, that Edison had his one brief encounter with formal education. At the one-room schoolhouse of the Rev. G.B. Engle, rote learning was central to the curriculum. So was corporal punishment, administered with a leather strap. It was a stifling environment, and Edison lasted

Thomas Edison's birthplace (opposite page, bottom), a modest brick house in Milan, Ohio. He spent the first seven years of his life there, until his father's financial setbacks compelled the family to move to Port Huron, Mich. Above, his parents, Samuel Edison Jr. and Nancy Elliott Edison.

just three miserable months, a period he always recalled with a shudder. "I was always at the foot of the class," Edison wrote much later. "I used to feel that the teachers did not sympathize with me and that my father thought I was stupid."

From that time forward, the future inventor was schooled by his mother. Nancy Edison had been a teacher at a small village school in Canada, and though her training was modest, she was genuinely literate. She read to her son from Shakespeare and Dickens and from enduring books like *The Decline and Fall of the Roman Empire* by Edward Gibbon and *The History of England* by the Scottish philosopher David Hume. Although Edison never entirely mastered spelling and grammar, he was fascinated by science. Just nine years old when his mother introduced him to his first science books, he promptly began performing primitive experiments at home, cluttering his bedroom with chemicals and wet cell batteries and then turning part of the family cellar into his first laboratory.

By the time he was 12, Edison had already tired of his home studies. What interested him was science and, more to the point, its practical applications. He was eager to get started in the world, and it was a world that had few objections to child labor. That year, he persuaded his mother to let him quit his home schooling to work as a newsboy, selling papers aboard a train that made a daily run between Port Huron and Detroit. (His father needed no convincing. He was the one who had spotted the job for his son and persuaded the railroad to give him a chance.) A year earlier, young Edison had made some money by growing vegetables in a small plot and selling them around Port Huron. Not long after he started with the railroad, he discovered he could expand that business by buying butter, fruits, and vegetables cheaply in Detroit and selling them for a profit in Port Huron. That led him to start a produce stand. Though not yet an inventor, he was already a budding businessman, one who was able to give his mother a dollar a day. Later, when he looked back on that period, Edison recalled: "The happiest time of my life was when I was 12 years old."

Edison had daily layovers in Detroit as he waited for the train to start its return trip to Port Huron, and these gave him a chance to deepen his reading. He joined the Detroit public library, where he discovered Isaac Newton and Victor Hugo—Hugo's novel *Les Misérables* would be a lifelong favorite—and countless manuals of applied science. The start of the Civil War in 1861 also created a hunger for news that Edison discovered he could turn to his profit. One of the war's bloodiest engagements was the Battle of Shiloh, fought in southwestern Tennessee over two days in April 1862. Knowing that people would be keen to get the latest word of developments in the fighting, Edison went to the offices of *The Detroit Free Press,* the paper he sold on the railroad, to get an advance look at the articles it planned to run. He then arranged to wire the headlines to stations along the route to Port Huron, alerting readers to the full-length stories coming their way. It was a stratagem that brought him a windfall in sales when he arrived at each station stop with the papers in hand.

Then came an even more ambitious idea. Why not produce and sell his own newspaper on board the train? With his profits from the Shiloh gambit, Edison bought a small printing press and 300 pounds of second-hand type. After teaching himself how to set the type, he launched *The Weekly Herald,* a paper he wrote and printed en route that was full of gossip, local news, railway schedules, and Edison's constant misspellings. Still intent on pursuing scientific experiments as well, he persuaded a conductor to let him set up a chemical laboratory at an unused end of the baggage and mail car, a project that nearly ended in disaster when a bottle of phosphorus broke

By the age of 12, Edison was helping to support his family by selling newspapers aboard the train that ran between Detroit and Port Huron. When the Civil War broke out, the industrious boy entrepreneur even launched his own newspaper, *The Weekly Herald* (below), which he wrote, printed, and sold on the train.

and set the car on fire. The conductor, furious, booted the boy inventor off the train, along with his laboratory and printing press.

It was not long after he started work on the railroad that Edison's lifelong difficulties with hearing began. He traced the problem to the day he was struggling to get on board a departing train and a well-meaning conductor lifted him into the car by his ears. "I felt something snap inside my head," he said. "And my deafness started from that time and has ever since progressed." One of his most thorough biographers, Matthew Josephson, doubts that Edison's problem could have stemmed from that incident, and believes the more likely source was repeated ear infections after an early bout of scarlet fever. Whatever the cause, for most of his life Edison was partially deaf. Although he could speak clearly and make out conversations when close enough to a speaker, it was a constant effort for him to understand what was being said in a crowded room.

Since he was prone to solitude from childhood, Edison's hearing difficulties probably led him to become even more inward, bookish, and devoted to his work. He saw the problem as, in some way, an advantage. It shut him off, he said, from "all the foolish conversation and meaningless sound that normal people hear." But it also meant the future inventor of the phonograph would struggle all his life to indulge his love of music. Music of any kind. As he confided once to his diary: "I haven't heard a bird sing since I was 12 years old."

By his teens, Edison was discovering himself. He knew that what truly fascinated him wasn't the grocery business or newspa-

Main St. in Salt Lake City, the site where the eastern and western lines of the transcontinental telegraph were joined on Oct. 24, 1861, a moment that symbolized the growing reach and importance of the telegraph industry that Edison entered the next year.

per publishing—it was telegraph equipment. Just three years before Edison's birth, Samuel Morse had tapped out his famous question—"What hath God wrought?"—opening the first permanent telegraph line between Washington, D.C., and Baltimore. Edison realized his deafness did not prevent him from hearing the click of the telegraph machine. He learned Morse code partly by hanging around telegraph offices and absorbing what he could, but also through lessons from a stationmaster, James Mackenzie, who owed him a profound debt of gratitude. Edison had saved the life of Mackenzie's young son, a toddler who was playing one day on a railway track, all the while unaware that a rolling boxcar was bearing down on him. Edison bolted from the station platform and carried the boy to safety. At Mackenzie's invitation, in the autumn of 1862, Edison came to live for a few months with him and his family to study telegraphy. Mackenzie was impressed that his new student arrived with telegraph equipment he had made himself at a gunsmith's shop.

By the 1860s, a freeform brotherhood of young men had emerged across America. They were itinerant telegraph operators, mobile technicians who had mastered Morse code and who moved from city to city to provide telegraphy services to whoever was paying. (The future steel tycoon Andrew Carnegie was one of them.) By the time he was 16, Edison was on his way to joining their ranks, working as a telegrapher at Stratford Junction, Ontario. But his career was almost cut short by a near tragedy. Directed to hold a freight train that was approaching his station—so as to keep the track clear for another train headed from the opposite direction—Edison discovered to his horror that the freight train had already left. It was barreling toward a head-on collision with the other train somewhere down the line. A crash was averted only because the engineers caught sight of one another in

Above left, a telegraph transmitter of the kind used in Edison's early years. At right, the New York operating room of Western Union. By the 1860s, Edison was a telegraph operator constantly looking to design improvements in the equipment he worked with.

time to brake. Edison and his stationmaster were summoned to an inquiry in Toronto and threatened with prison time for dereliction of duty under Canadian law. Edison escaped that fate by ducking quietly out of the inquiry and making a getaway aboard a freight train that brought him back safely to Michigan.

Over the next several years, Edison bounced from job to job in telegraph stations across America, with stops in Fort Wayne and Indianapolis, as well as Cincinnati, Memphis, Louisville, and finally Boston. Although he gained a reputation as a fast "receiver," able to take down Morse code messages in his efficient, no-frills handwriting, Edison was dismissed from one job after another for neglecting his official duties while he tinkered with some new invention, usually one aimed at making telegraph communication faster or more accurate. He lived in cheap boarding houses, his rooms cluttered with half-finished inventions, pocket tools, and scavenged materials—wire coils, battery cells, sheets of metal—that he toted from place to place in the expectation they might be useful in his next bout of inspiration.

After more than five years of this peripatetic life, Edison needed a change. It plainly wasn't enough anymore to be a telegraph operator. He wanted to devote himself full time to advancing the technology of telegraphy. One impetus to his new conviction was his discovery of *Experimental Researches in Electricity*, a work by the eminent English scientist Michael Faraday. Edison was thrilled by the book, which gave him his most coherent account yet of the workings of electricity.

Having spent more than a year in Boston employed by Western Union, he quit his job. In January 1869, a notice appeared in the pages of a small telegraph trade journal. It announced that the former telegraph operator Thomas A. Edison "would hereafter devote his full time to bringing out his inventions." He had made his move. From that moment on, he would commit himself to one of the world's most arduous but romantic occupations. He would be an inventor.

DOTS, DASHES & DOLLARS

CHAPTER TWO

As it turned out, to become an independent inventor would require more of Edison than simply placing a newspaper announcement. First there was the matter of developing a modicum of business sense. It would be a long process. In the summer of 1869, Edison was granted the first of the staggering 1,093 U.S. patents that he would claim over the course of his lifetime. Not all of them turned out to be technological successes, and even the first to qualify in that way still proved to be a commercial failure. It was a mechanical vote counter that Edison, along with a Boston investor who had advanced him $100, hoped would appeal to legislative bodies. By equipping each lawmaker's desk with "yes" and "no" buttons wired to a tote board at the front of the chamber, it would allow them to make quick tabulations of floor votes. But to Edison's surprise, when he brought his new system to the Massachusetts state legislature, and then

A portrait of the soon-to-be-legendary inventor in his early 20s.

 19

to Congress itself, he learned that a quick tabulation was the last thing legislators wanted. In any vote, the losing side preferred a slow head count that gave it time to round up more support. And every elected official knew that at some point he'd be on the losing side of a vote.

The failure of his vote tabulator taught Edison a valuable lesson. He vowed that in future he would only work on inventions for which there was a demand. And one market he knew he could count on was businessmen anxious to get faster information that could help them turn a profit. At a time when the telegraph was the fastest means of communication throughout America, Edison saw his best hope for personal gain in working to find improvements that might make telegraphy even faster or adaptable for new uses. To that end, he soon developed a mechanical stock ticker that received stock prices by telegraph and printed them on a moving paper tape. It worked well enough to attract about 30 subscribers among brokerage offices. But when Edison's financial backers sold his patent rights to a large telegraph company, he got almost nothing from the sale. Then there was his disappointing trial of a "duplex" telegraph transmitter. Had it worked properly, it would have been able to send more than one message down a single wire, doubling the number of transmissions a telegraph company could handle each day. But in its first demonstration the duplex failed, leaving Edison $800 in debt to another of his backers.

Casting about for a lifeline, Edison decided to quit Boston and try his luck in New York City. In the spring of 1869, he borrowed a few dollars for steamship fare and arrived in New York with his pockets empty. But before long he found his way to Franklin L. Pope, an electrical engineer and telegrapher. Pope worked for the Gold Indicator Co., a firm based in lower Manhattan that provided a wire transmission service to brokers which kept them abreast of changes in the price of gold. Pope suggested that while Edison looked for a job, he could sleep on a cot in the company's offices. Edison leapt at the offer. Over the next several days, while subsisting on a diet of apple dumplings and coffee, he also took the opportunity to acquaint himself with the firm's central transmitting device. A good thing, too. When the machine abruptly malfunctioned one day, causing the firm's operations to shut down, Edison was able to spot the problem and fix it. The company's grateful leader offered him a job managing and improving the transmitter at a higher salary than he had ever made. Just 22 years old, the penniless inventor who had only 12 weeks of formal schooling was now a well-paid engineer. When Pope left the firm a few months later, Edison was promoted to his job for a phenomenal $300 a month.

The tumultuous world of 19th-century capitalism being what it was, the Gold Indicator Co. was shortly absorbed by Western Union. Although Edison was invited to stay on, he chose instead to form a partnership with Pope to design and build telegraphic machinery and provide electrical engineering services. Rooming at Pope's home in Elizabeth, N.J., he set to work producing an improved gold price transmitter. It turned out to be so successful that Western Union decided to buy out the pair rather than tolerate a potential competitor. Edison realized $5,000 from the deal, which allowed him to write home to his father in triumph: "Don't do any hard work, and get mother anything she desires. You can draw on me for money."

But by 1870, Edison had dissolved his partnership with Pope and accepted a job as an engineer with Western Union, where he would make a series of improvements on telegraphic equipment. One was for an improved stock ticker that brought him a bonus of a breathtaking $30,000. (He had been thinking of asking for $5,000.) Now he truly had the cash to go into business for himself.

Gold trading in New York's financial district, as illustrated by an engraving of the action on Sept. 24, 1869, the year Edison arrived in the city. He soon found a job maintaining and improving the equipment for a company that transmitted up-to-the-minute gold prices to buyers and sellers. At left, a stock ticker patented by Edison in 1872.

In Edison's time, office romances were not uncommon, and in his Newark shop he kept close to 16-year-old employee Mary Stilwell, pictured here about a year after the two wed on Christmas Day, 1871.

(And to buy a silk top hat and a Prince Albert coat.) When Western Union gave him a half-million-dollar contract to produce 1,200 of his stock tickers, he found space on the top floor of a warehouse on Ward St. in Newark, N.J., equipped it with machinery, and established his first laboratory/workshop. Supervising a crew that would eventually number 50 craftsmen and machinists, Edison spent the next five years at Ward St. and a series of other workshops, dreaming up and producing all kinds of new electrical equipment.

But first there would be a melancholy mission home. In April 1871, Edison returned to Port Huron for the first time in three years for the funeral of his mother, who had died after years of poor health. Home held few attractions for him now, and he stayed just briefly before hurrying back to his new business in Newark. His 67-year-old father was apparently in a hurry, too. Within a few weeks he had taken up with a 17-year-old farm girl. He would soon marry her, presenting Edison with a step-mother seven years younger than himself, and one who would eventually bear three children by his elderly father.

Perhaps his father's abrupt remarriage prompted Edison to realize that it was time for him to be thinking about marriage, too. He soon had a candidate. Mary Stilwell was a 16-year-old employee in his shop. Having little experience of women, Edison developed the unnerving habit of standing over her as she worked. As he recalled later, his partial deafness worked to his advantage. It gave him permission "for getting a little closer to her than I would have dared...to hear her. If something had not overcome my natural bashfulness, I might have been too faint of heart to win."

One day he suddenly asked her: "What do you think of me, little girl? Do you like me?" Then he added: "Don't be in a hurry about telling me, unless you would like to marry me." When she expressed surprise at this turn in the conversation, he replied simply: "Think it over, talk to your mother about it, and let me know as soon as convenient—Tuesday, say." They were married on Christmas Day, 1871, in Newark. An anxious and insecure Mary insisted that her older sister Alice accompany them on their honeymoon.

Edison and his new bride would live in Newark, attended by servants, in a house that he bought just a few days before their wedding. Within a year, Mary gave birth to a daughter, Marion. Ever the devoted telegrapher, Edison impishly took to calling her "Dot." In the same vein, after a son, Thomas Jr., was born in 1876, Edison started calling him "Dash." A second son, William Leslie, arrived two years later, but there were no telegraphic nicknames left to give him.

Edison's children, like his wife, grew accustomed to their father's long working hours. Pictured here, in photographs from around 1883, are his daughter, Marion, and sons, William and Thomas, Jr.

The new Mrs. Edison soon realized that she had to accommodate to her husband's tireless work habits. He was often at his lab until all hours, engrossed in some new problem. According to one story, a friend once found him there late at night, half asleep at his desk. When he told Edison it was midnight and time to go home, the relentless inventor was surprised to hear the hour. "I must go home then," he agreed sleepily. "I was married today." Dot would later recall that her mother often gave parties that her busy father didn't attend.

As is typical with technological advances, Edison's inventions weren't usually bursts from the blue but improvements, sometimes important ones, on devices that had already begun to evolve in the hands of other inventors. That was true of one of the biggest breakthroughs of his early career, the automatic telegraph, a machine that used perforated paper tapes, not unlike the rolls in old player pianos, to send and receive messages at much faster rates than a key operator could

Below, Edison's 1873 patented version of a printing telegraph, a device that printed messages in words instead of Morse code. At right, traders run from the New York Stock Exchange amid the panic on Sept. 18, 1873, the start of a long economic downturn in which Edison's fortunes also suffered.

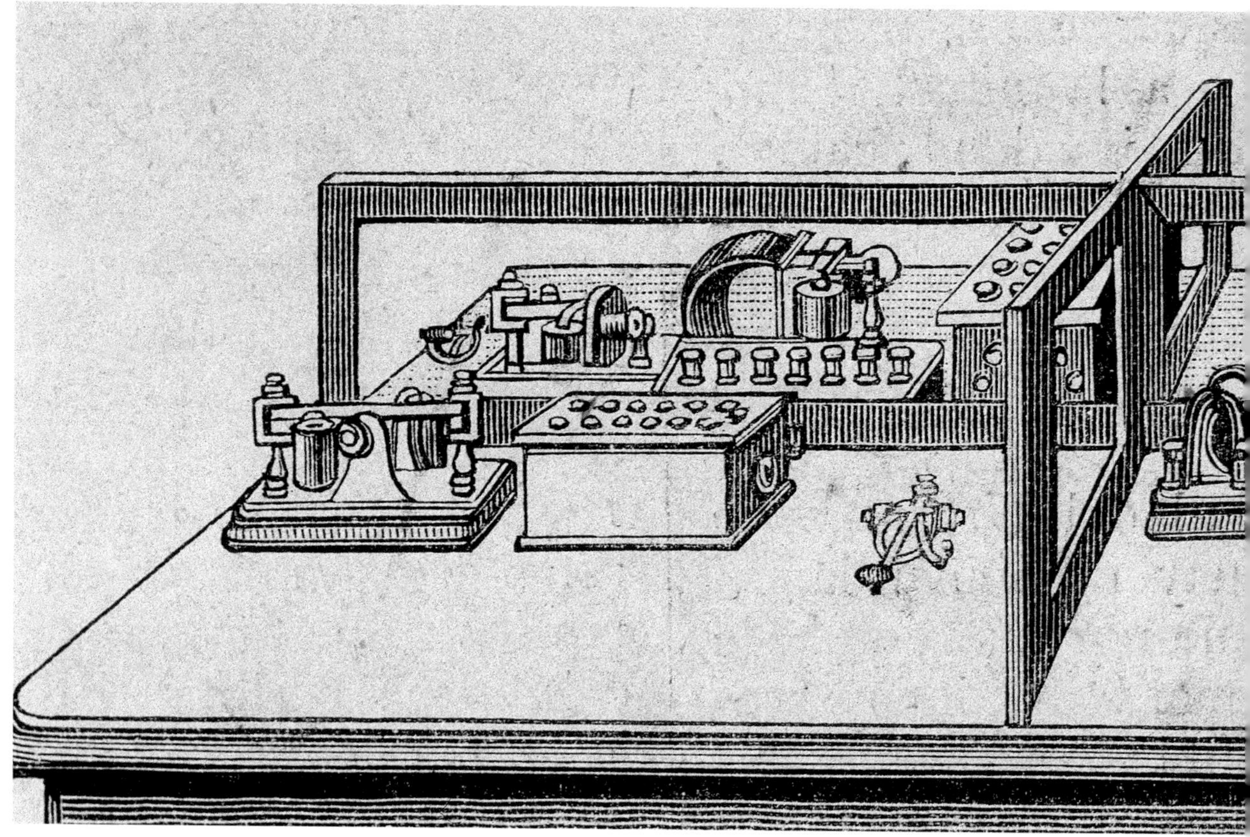

do by hand. It was first developed by a man named George D. Little. In 1871, financiers who were partners in a firm called the Automatic Telegraph Co. advanced Edison $40,000 to improve Little's machine. By the winter of 1873, Edison had arrived at a much more workable model. Just then, the shadowy financier Jay Gould, a man notorious for his stock manipulations and other clandestine financial dealings, took over Automatic Telegraph. Gould's primary holdings were in railways, but by that year he was ready to pick a fight with Western Union. To that end, he arranged for Edison's automatic telegraphic lines to be strung along the rights of way of railway lines he owned, presenting Western Union with a direct challenge to its near monopoly of the telegraph system.

In these same years Edison was also engrossed once more in the solution to the problem of moving more than one message down a telegraph wire, the breakthrough in "duplex" telegraphy that had eluded him earlier. But as he struggled to solve it, as part of a working agreement with Western Union, the financial panic of 1873 got under way. Wall Street firms shuddered and fell, and with them the telegraph businesses that depended on them for clients. In the spring of that year, when Edison was demonstrating his automatic telegraph to postal authorities in London, his wife found herself fending off the sheriff in Newark, who was threatening to shut down Edison's Ward St. workshop and sell off his equipment to satisfy his creditors. Soon after Edison returned to the U.S. in June—without making a sale to the British—he was forced to sell his house and move his family into an apartment. For a time, his arrangement with Western Union to pursue work on duplex telegraphy also fell victim to the general economic collapse.

In the midst of this turmoil Edison somehow managed to continue focusing on work. One new

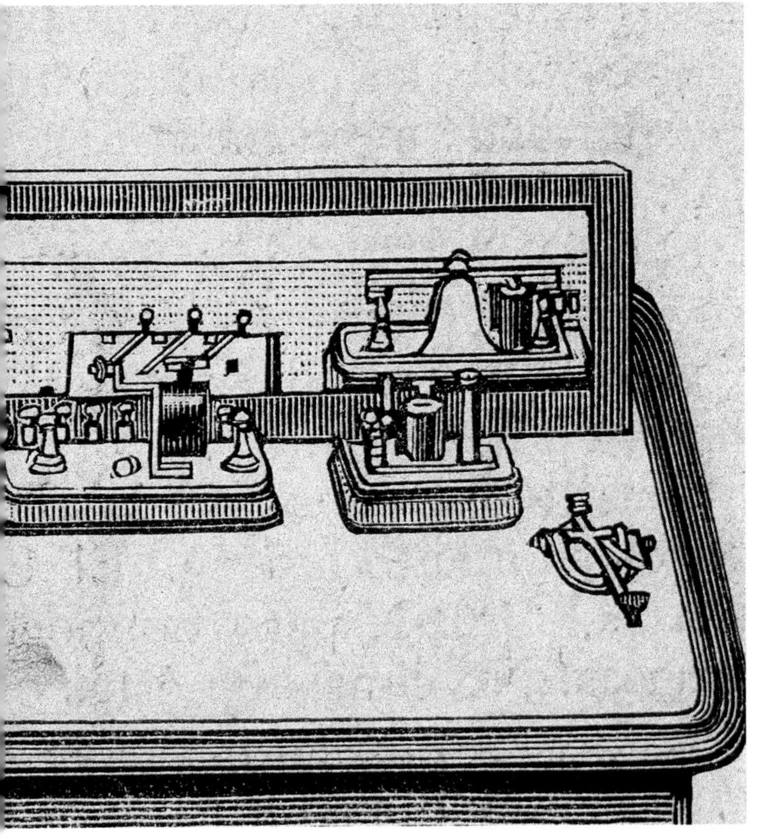

Edison's 1874 Quadruplex Telegraph, at left, which could send and receive four messages simultaneously on a single wire, put him in the middle of a lengthy court battle between his frequent employer, Western Union, and his sometime financier, railroad tycoon Jason "Jay" Gould, above.

invention of 1874 was a battery-operated electric pen, which permitted the user to produce multiple copies of any document. Although it proved to be unwieldy and was a commercial failure, it was a forerunner of the mimeograph machine that was the standard office copier before the invention of photocopying. At about the same time, Edison also renewed his arrangement with Western Union to work on multiplex telegraphy. By the summer he had perfected a "quadruplex" device that could send not one but two messages in opposite directions at the same time. Western Union agreed to buy the patent rights Edison held jointly with its chief engineer, George B. Prescott. Soon the company was installing the new device along its telegraph lines. But there was a complication. Late in 1874, Edison had also accepted a payment of $30,000 directly from Gould for Edison's 50% ownership rights to the quadruplex. A welter of complex lawsuits ensued, as both sides struggled to claim ownership of Edison's immensely valuable invention. In 1881, Gould emerged the winner. By that time Edison, who had been promised further profits by Gould that he never saw, was part of a lengthy group lawsuit against the financier. It dragged through the courts until 1906—almost 30 years—and when it was over it netted the plaintiffs exactly one dollar in damages.

Of course, by 1906, Edison was a world-famous inventor who had long since put the quadruplex affair behind him and found a way to put his $30,000 from Gould to good use. In 1875, not long after receiving the money, he decided to shut down the last of his several workshops in Newark. He had in mind to move out to the New Jersey countryside, where he wanted to build a large, sophisticated lab complex. He commissioned his father to find a suitable location. Soon they had one, a tiny hamlet about 25 miles southwest of New York. It was called Menlo Park.

MENLO PARK: THE WIZARD'S LAND OF OZ

It has been called "the first industrial research laboratory in America, or in the world," the forerunner of the R&D labs that would be built in the next century by General Electric and Bell, by Microsoft, Apple, and Google. When it went into operation in the spring of 1876, the U.S. had few labs of any kind, and those were mostly connected to major institutions like the Massachusetts Institute of Technology. But when Edison first set eyes on the microscopic village of Menlo Park, N.J., the place where he would plant his pioneering operation on 34 acres, it was mostly just empty land and the remains of a failed real estate scheme. No more than six houses dotted the barren landscape. The largest of them, standing near the railway line leading from New York to Philadelphia, had served for a while as the office and salesroom for lots that never sold.

Edison would choose that place as a home for himself and his family. Nearby, he had his father build the two-story frame structure, 100 feet long by 30 feet wide, that served as his "invention factory" for the next five years. Over time, as his fame exploded, the site became a pilgrimage spot for journalists and worshipful visitors, venerated as the place where Edison created the phonograph and the light bulb, the magical seat of the Wizard of Menlo Park.

Since it was the first workspace he would own outright, instead of renting from landlords, Edison could lay out the new main building as he pleased. The first floor held a reception room, office, library, and storeroom. The upper floor was a single large room with workbenches, machinery, and glass cases filled with materials and jars full of chemicals. He had boundless ambitions for his new facility. It would not be a pure science lab like the one at the Smithsonian Institution, but a place to develop products, innovations for the marketplace. And as he told a friend, he planned to produce " a minor invention every 10 days, and a big thing every six months or so."

Many of Edison's regular crew from Newark relocated to Menlo Park as well. They included his British-born chief assistant, Charles

The Menlo Park lab in 1880, with Edison seated left of center. The gaslight ceiling fixtures had already been replaced by Edison's new electric light bulbs.

Batchelor; John Kruesi, a Swiss clockmaker adept at building machines of any kind; and John Ott, a mechanic who had scored his job by briskly reassembling a stock ticker that Edison put before him in a heap of disconnected pieces. Batchelor and Kruesi, who were both married, lived with their families in two of the smaller houses in the compound. For the single men Edison established a boarding house run by the widow of one of his Newark employees. The only other building of consequence was a saloon near the train station with a billiard table. There wasn't much to do in Menlo Park but work. That was how Edison liked it.

As always, Edison put in long hours, sometimes working into the morning. When he did, his crew was expected to do the same. There was a regular midnight supper provided, and sometimes Mrs. Edison came by with more of a feast, which gave her a welcome opportunity to socialize. Edison loved the isolation of Menlo Park; it let him work in peace. But his wife, who had grown up in a large town, found it trying. On many weekends, she gathered up the children and took them back to Newark for visits with her family.

Although Edison's name is forever associated with Menlo Park, he worked there for just five years before moving to New York in 1881 to further his plan to electrify the city. By 1887, he had built a much larger laboratory in West Orange, N.J., having long since closed the old place for good. Over time, the abandoned buildings would sink into ruin. Some even burned, as his former house did in 1914.

Others were stripped for their salvageable material—the fate of his lab—though all the while a bustling town was growing up around the dwindling remains. Eventually the very name would disappear, but for a worthy cause. In 1954, in honor of the man who put it on the map, Menlo Park, N.J., was officially renamed Edison. And today the little village that once played host to an invention factory is the fifth-largest city in the state.

At top, the Menlo Park compound as it appeared in 1881. The long building at center left is the lab, behind it is the machine shop, and between them a small glass-blowing house. Above, Edison's men on the front porches of the lab; at right, an experimental electric train that ran on the grounds.

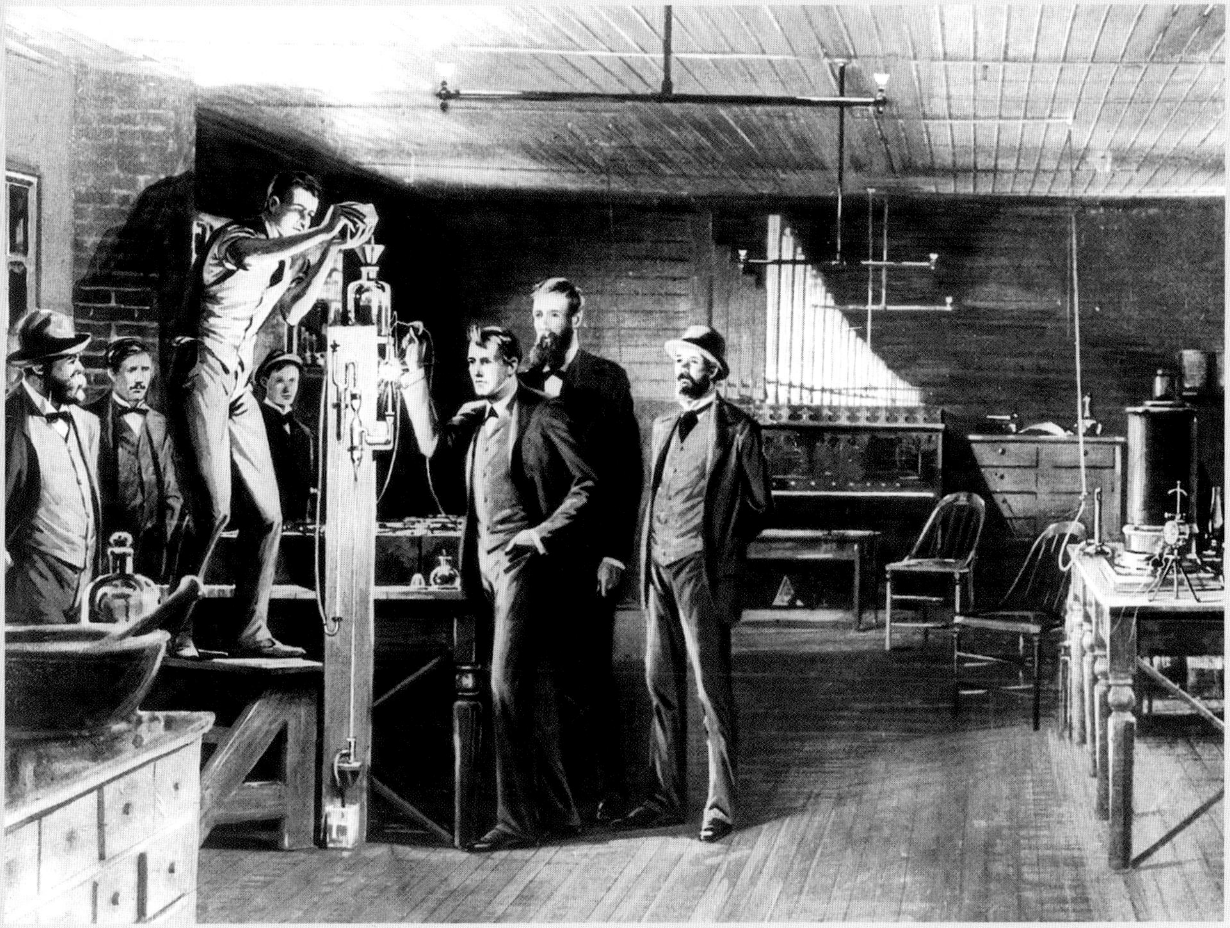

THE DAILY GRAPHIC

An Illustrated Evening Newspaper.

39 & 41 PARK PLACE

Clockwise from top: working on the light bulb, Edison and his men experiment with mercury; in 1925, reading a new Menlo Park plaque honoring his work; a magazine illustration celebrates "the Wizard."

THE TALKING MACHINE

CHAPTER THREE

Though Edison had once promised "a big thing every six months or so" from his lab at Menlo Park, in its first year of operation what he and his men produced were mostly small things. An electric jewelry-engraving machine and another for shearing sheep were not inventions likely to make a man rich and famous. But one problem that Edison continued to pursue did have that potential: how to squeeze ever more messages down a single telegraph wire.

A promising line of inquiry was sound telegraphy. An "acoustic telegraph" being investigated by Alexander Graham Bell and others could send and receive multiple tones produced by a tuning fork or reed. Elisha Gray, a Western Union electrical engineer, had coined the term "telephone" to describe a device he invented that could transmit as many as 16 different notes. From there it was a short step to the possibility that the human voice might be

Edison poses proudly with his new phonograph in an 1878 portrait made by the studio of Mathew Brady.

sent along a wire. Bell, a Scottish immigrant working in Salem, Mass., was investigating that very idea. His approach was to use a metal disk that vibrated in response to spoken sounds and then transmitted the vibrations along a wire to another device that translated them back into speech. In the summer of 1875, Bell completed a crude working model. By the following February, he had applied for a patent for an improved version.

A replica of Edison's first phonograph, with its foil-covered cylinder and two brass heads, one for recording, one for playing back. Below left, the *Scientific American* article that first described it to the world.

With the support of a contract with Western Union, Edison had been tinkering with his own ideas about how to transmit voices. In the summer of 1876, when Bell's telephone was the sensation of the Centennial Exhibition in Philadelphia, Western Union urged Edison to see what he could do to make an improved version for the company. Eventually he came up with a carbon transmitter that conveyed voices far more clearly than Bell's first invention. It was, in effect, the first microphone, and one that worked so well it was used in telephone mouthpieces for decades. At the same time, he produced an improved receiver that, as an unexpected dividend, proved capable of playing music with surprising clarity.

Edison still didn't think of it as a phonograph, and it wasn't. It didn't record or play back recordings. It was effectively no more than a telephone that could broadcast music, but even that was enough to amaze and entertain crowds. Bell was already showing paying audiences how his phone could be placed on a stage and fill a hall with music being played in another room miles away. Even before Edison completed work on his carbon transmitter, in the summer of 1877, an audience of 3,500 in Philadelphia had been treated to an early version of his phone doing the same thing.

All along, however, Edison remained focused on the problem of audio telegraphy. It was possible now for a telegraph operator to send his message by voice down a wire to an operator on the other end. But that operator would then have to copy out the message by hand. What if there were some way to automatically record the vocal message on the receiving end? This was the question that preoccupied Edison in the summer of 1877. The breakthrough came on July 18, after one of the midnight suppers that he often shared in his laboratory with his men. At the time, they were experimenting with many different materials for the telephone diaphragm—the surface inside a phone's mouthpiece that vibrates when sounds strike it. On that night, it occurred to Edison that if a needle were attached to the diaphragm, it would move with the vibrations and could inscribe the movements as jittery lines onto a moving surface of some kind, perhaps wax paper. Then, if the paper were pulled back, with the needle still resting in the lines it had inscribed, perhaps it might move the diaphragm to repeat the same vibrations and thus the same sounds.

Would it? Within an hour, his assistants had rigged up a test model, using wax paper attached to a roller as

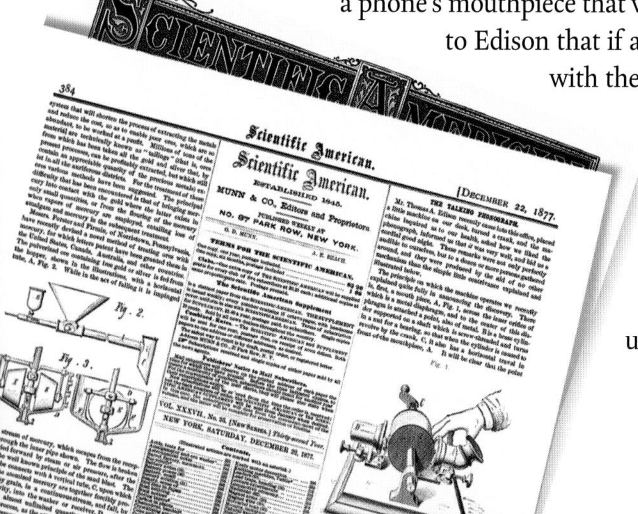

Scientific American

384

Scientific American.

[DECEMBER 22, 1877.

Scientific American.

ESTABLISHED 1845.

MUNN & CO., Editors and Proprietors.

PUBLISHED WEEKLY AT

NO. 37 PARK ROW, NEW YORK.

THE TALKING PHONOGRAPH.

VOL. XXXVII., No. 25. [New Series.]

NEW YORK, SATURDAY, DECEMBER 22, 1877.

the surface. Edison leaned forward and spoke the words: "Mary had a little lamb." When the paper was pulled back, the speaker sounded the words again, or almost. "Ary ad ell amb." Not perfect, but not bad.

In fact, it was the beginning of a revolution, though it wouldn't immediately dawn on Edison that he had discovered something the world was waiting for. But the world would let him know soon enough. In November, *Scientific American* published a letter from one of Edison's men describing the peculiar new discovery. That alone was enough to trigger a flood of excited speculation in the press.

By that month, Edison's assistant John Kruesi had built a working model of the phonograph in iron and brass. It substituted tin foil for the wax paper, which was wrapped around a three-and-a half-inch cylinder turned by a hand crank. In December, Edison and two assistants brought it to the New York offices of *Scientific American.* With a dozen or so people gathered around, they set the machine on a desk. One of them turned the crank while Edison spoke into it. Then they played his words back. The little box asked the assembled audience: "How do you do? How do you like the phonograph?"

They liked it very much indeed. An enthusiastic article describing the scene appeared in the next edition of *Scientific American.* And with that, Edison became an international celebrity. Reporters and writers from all around the U.S. flocked to Menlo Park to witness

How It Worked

Edison inscribed sound so it could be stored and replayed.

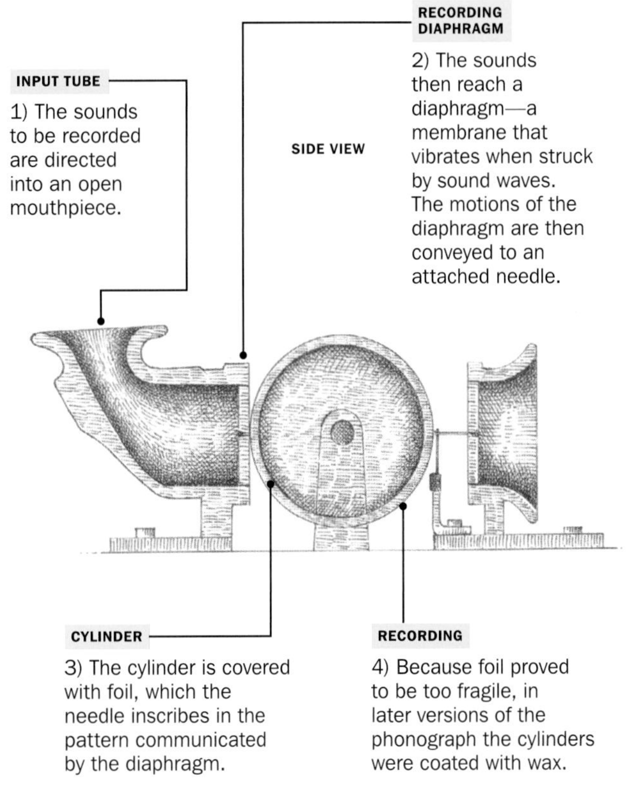

RECORDING DIAPHRAGM
2) The sounds then reach a diaphragm—a membrane that vibrates when struck by sound waves. The motions of the diaphragm are then conveyed to an attached needle.
INPUT TUBE
1) The sounds to be recorded are directed into an open mouthpiece.
SIDE VIEW
CYLINDER
3) The cylinder is covered with foil, which the needle inscribes in the pattern communicated by the diaphragm.
RECORDING
4) Because foil proved to be too fragile, in later versions of the phonograph the cylinders were coated with wax.

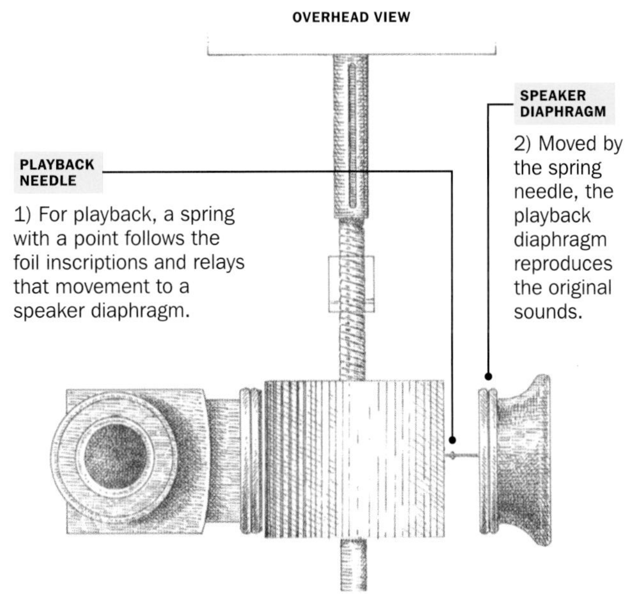

OVERHEAD VIEW
SPEAKER DIAPHRAGM
2) Moved by the spring needle, the playback diaphragm reproduces the original sounds.
PLAYBACK NEEDLE
1) For playback, a spring with a point follows the foil inscriptions and relays that movement to a speaker diaphragm.

the miracle of the talking machine and to outdo one another in composing tributes to the modest young genius with the rumpled clothes and the haystack of unruly hair. "The greatest inventor of the age," they called him, "the New Jersey Columbus." Or as one headline put it: "A Man of Thirty-One Revolutionizing the Whole World." One reporter asked Edison admiringly if he wasn't "a good deal of a wizard." Oh no, he objected, "I don't believe much in that sort of thing." But the name stuck. Now, he would now always be "The Wizard of Menlo Park."

His reputation went global. Scientific minds in England and France marveled at news of the little device and proclaimed its inventor no mere "mechanic" but a true scientist, a man who discovered principles, not just gadgets. In Paris, where the phonograph was an object of fascination at the Universal Exhibition of 1878, paying crowds packed a hall three times a day to hear it play.

Edison hadn't sought fame, but he didn't avoid it. He entertained the constant stream of visitors to his laboratory by whistling popular tunes into his machine, then letting it whistle them back, or sneezing and having it do likewise. On April 18, he traveled to Washington, D.C., where he demonstrated his phonograph first to members of Congress gathered at a private home, then to President Rutherford B. Hayes at the White House. Meanwhile, Alexander Graham Bell, knowing that he had very nearly invented the same machine first, looked on from the sidelines in dismay. "It is a most astonishing thing to me," he said, "that I could possibly have let this invention slip through my fingers."

Yet Edison still had no clear idea of just what it was he had made. To be sure, he hoped his new invention had commercial possibilities. As he told one reporter, the phonograph "is my baby, and I expect it to grow up and be a big feller and support me in my old age." His phonograph company established an exhibition business, training men to demonstrate the machine's ability to play music at public performances that cost 25 cents per customer. But while he understood that the device could be used to play music, he didn't yet realize that this was to be its real destiny. It didn't help that, though he loved music and had strong opinions on it—hated Wagner, loved Beethoven—his near deafness made it a struggle for him to hear it. In later years, because his inner ear could still pick up vibrations that his middle and outer ear could not, he sometimes knelt down and bit the wood of a phonograph case or even a piano leg to "hear" through his teeth what was being played.

Edison thought of the phonograph initially as a toy, and accordingly, the first uses he considered for it were in playthings—a talking doll, a train that whistled and chugged. He also believed that its real future was as an office machine, one that would allow businessmen to dictate letters that their secretaries could play back and transcribe later. But with a $10,000 advance from a group of investors organized as the Edison Speaking Phonograph Co., Edison set to work perfecting a version of his machine for the consumer market. To his investors that meant one thing only: a music box. American cities were growing, and with them a new market for leisure activities and entertainment.

This mass market was new territory for Edison. Most of his previous inventions had been aimed solely at business customers, like brokerage firms or telegraph companies. And it took a lot to make the phonograph a workable product even for them. Each tinfoil recording carried no more than a minute's worth of sound and could be played only a few times before it disintegrated. Edison toyed for a while with various fixes but never succeeded in making a product ready for market. On a sudden whim, in July he went off with a professor friend on an extended trip west to observe a solar eclipse from the best vantage point in Wyoming, and to test a new invention, the

Although we think of him as a lone genius, what made Edison a truly modern inventor was that he transformed his inspirations into realities with a team. Three of his most important assistants were, from left, John Kruesi, a Swiss clockmaker and machinist who often produced the working models of Edison's ideas; John Ott, a nimble mechanic; and Charles Batchelor, who had worked in the textile mills of Manchester, England.

"tasimeter," an ultrasensitive thermometer. And then, remarkably, on his return, he put the phonograph aside for almost 10 years while he devoted himself to a true obsession—perfecting electric light and power.

By the time he returned to the baby that was also his problem child, in 1887, Edison had shut down Menlo Park and moved to working quarters in New York City. In the fall of that year, he moved again, this time to a much larger new laboratory/workshop in West Orange, N.J. He was spurred to action by the realization that serious competitors had entered the field. Two years earlier, none other than Alexander Graham Bell, teamed with his cousin Chichester and a technician, Charles Sumner Tainter, who was the principal inventor, had come up with what they called the "graphophone." It replaced Edison's flimsy tinfoil cylinder with a more durable one covered with wax, and it had a loosely mounted "floating" stylus that was more sensitive to the grooves it was following. It was also powered by a treadle designed to give steadier motion to the turning cylinder and so produce a less fluctuating sound.

Mindful of the magic of Edison's name, Bell and Tainter offered to go into partnership with him to manufacture their machine, but Edison wouldn't hear of it. As he told his London representative, he wanted nothing to do with Bell or "his phonograph pronounced backward." Prodded into action, he turned his attention to his sound machine in the spring of 1887, initially with his chief assistant, Charles Batchelor, as his principal collaborator. Once his West Orange lab was ready that fall, it was possible to divide his enlarged crew into teams that could focus separately on different aspects of the problem. One set to work finding the best wax for the recording cylinders, another figuring out how to duplicate recordings for mass production, another working on the motor and battery, and so forth. In all, 120 lab workers would be involved. But it wasn't until June 16, 1888, after a marathon effort over three sleepless days and nights, that Edison arrived at a version he was willing to offer to the public. A widely publicized photograph taken of him right afterward—accompanied by the inflated claim that it showed him after five sleepless nights, not three—presented him as an almost manically dedicated inventor, slumped sideways beside his new device, mouth turned down, dark circles under eyes that looked slightly dazed. His resemblance to another world conqueror, Napoleon, was much noted.

Edison in a photo taken in June 1888, following a marathon work session over three sleepless days and nights, during which he and his team completed work on the improved version of his phonograph.

Edison's new phonograph had elements in common with Bell and Tainter's. It too used wax cylinders and had a more sensitive stylus. But while in most eyes it was the superior machine, it would be hitting the market 18 months after theirs. A former glassware manufacturer, Jesse Lippincott, had already formed a business, the North American Phonograph Co., to market and distribute their product. Edison hoped to produce his through a company under his personal control. But when he arranged to demonstrate an early version of the improved machine to a group of potential investors, the show was a bust. At the last minute, a well-meaning Edison employee swapped out a crucial part, causing the machine to badly underperform for its crucial audience, which drifted away in disappointment.

As a fallback, Edison cut his own deal to supply thousands of his new phonographs to Lippincott to market along with the Bell/Tainter graphophone by renting them to business customers. To produce the machines, Edison had already built an entire factory next to the West Orange lab. Like Edison, Lippincott was primarily interested in the phonograph as a dictation machine. Edison developed a version designed specially for that market. What he would eventually call the "Ediphone" had a mouthpiece at the end of a long rubber tube so that the user could speak into it in a normal tone of voice. The same tube would serve as a listening device when the recording was played back, somewhat like a headphone.

But even the "perfected" phonograph, as Edison called it, had serious problems. The wax cylinders could only hold two minutes of speech or music, too little time for most songs or business. The cylin-

While Edison's original phonograph was produced in small numbers, his improved device was widely available and put to many purposes. At far left, an Edison delivery van; near left, a secretary uses the business version to type from pre-recorded dictation. Below left, a surgeon uses the machine to record notes on a patient; below right, a native of American Samoa records his voice.

ders were also still fragile, and the cylinders and battery that ran the machine required constant adjustment and maintenance to work properly. Clerks and secretaries resisted the complicated device, and the Ediphone sold poorly. Even Edison didn't use it. Thousands of faulty phonographs were also returned to the factory, seriously straining Lippincott's finances, especially since he was suffering similar problems with the Bell/Tainter graphophone. By 1891, he had suffered a stroke and died.

Even as his phonograph was floundering, Edison made the rash decision to follow through on an idea he had considered but put aside a decade earlier: to produce talking dolls. Because the vocals for each doll had to be recorded separately, Edison arranged for hundreds of girls to come to his West Orange factory to record nursery rhymes. Three thousand of the dolls were ready by the spring of 1890, but they turned out to be a fiasco. In nearly all of them, the delicate sound mechanisms were damaged in transit. By April, Edison had withdrawn them from sale.

In the 1890s, Edison's sales benefited from the rise of phonograph parlors. The forerunners of videogame arcades, these were public places where customers could play favorite songs or comedy recordings by inserting a coin into a machine, then placing rubber listening tubes into their ears like modern earbuds. Meanwhile, however, more competitors were crowding around. The newly formed Columbia Phonograph Co., an ancestor of today's CBS, was mass-producing recorded mu-

WAXING ELOQUENT: THE EVOLUTION OF THE PHONOGRAPH

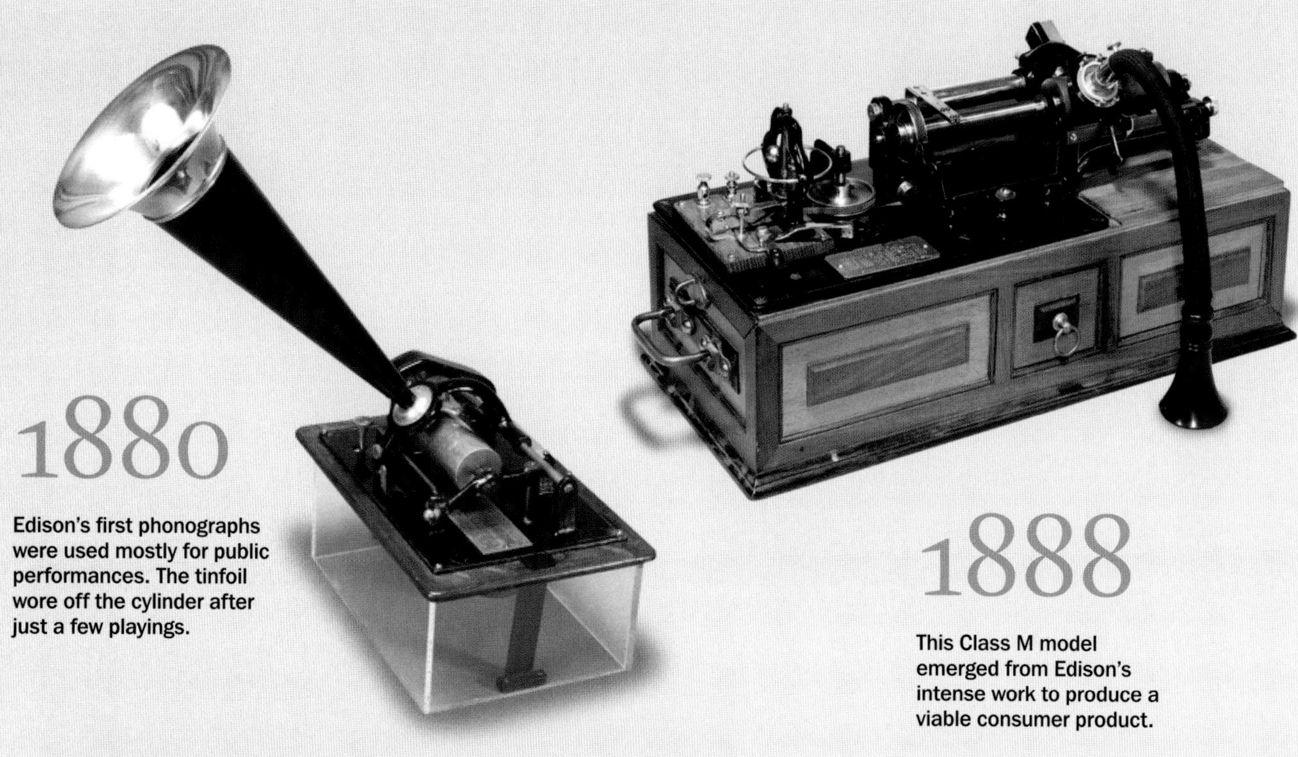

1880

Edison's first phonographs were used mostly for public performances. The tinfoil wore off the cylinder after just a few playings.

1888

This Class M model emerged from Edison's intense work to produce a viable consumer product.

1909

The Fireside was designed to play both two-minute wax cylinders and Edison's new four-minute variety.

1902

A new manufacturing process for Gold Moulded cylinders made it possible to press numerous copies.

In the years following Edison's invention of the phonograph in 1877, his new machine and its recordings went through many changes, especially after he set to work in the late 1880s on a much improved version.

1896

Edison's Home Phonograph was one of the first manufactured for household use, instead of as an office machine.

1899

The all-metal Gem was Edison's response to the demand for a less expensive model. It could play but not record.

1911

To compete with the Victrola, Edison's Amberola was designed as a piece of furniture

1912

By this year, although he continued to sell cylinders, Edison finally began to produce records. This label is from the 1920s.

In a photograph taken around 1900, Edison, at center, listens to a piano being recorded through the giant horn of an Edison phonograph custom-built to produce music for the commercial market.

AUTOMATIC

sic cylinders. Around 1895, Emile Berliner entered the field with his "gramophone," a machine that played records—flat circular discs that were easier to use and store than bulky cylinders. To supply his machines with products to play, Berliner's company also signed musical artists to make recordings.

By 1901, an even more serious contender came along. From the aftermath of a welter of lawsuits involving the collapse of Berliner's company, the Victor Co. emerged with its popular "Victrola." This product domesticated the phonograph by hiding its large metal sounding horn inside a wooden cabinet, transforming it from a machine into a piece of fine furniture. Over the years, and even more aggressively than its predecessor, Victor would sign recording deals with famous musicians and conductors, such as Jascha Heifetz, Fritz Kreisler, and Arturo Toscanini, and opera singers like Nellie Melba and the hugely popular Italian tenor Enrico Caruso, whose already sizable following his recordings would make larger.

All the same, as the 20th century opened Edison's phonograph and recording businesses were finally profitable, even helping to finance his investigations into ideas such as automobile storage batteries and concrete houses. But maybe he loved his baby too well. As the public's preference for records became ever more clear, Edison insisted on manufacturing cylinders. In his opinion, and that of many other people, they produced superior sound. Not until 1912, when the Victor Co.'s business was plainly overtaking his, did he relent. Even then he insisted on producing a higher-fidelity recording surface—what would come to be called "hi-fi." In a foreshadowing of the videocassette format war decades later between Betamax and VHS, his records couldn't be played on phonographs manufactured by his competitors.

In the 1890s, coin-operated phonograph arcades became popular as a way for people who did not own their own players to hear favorite recordings.

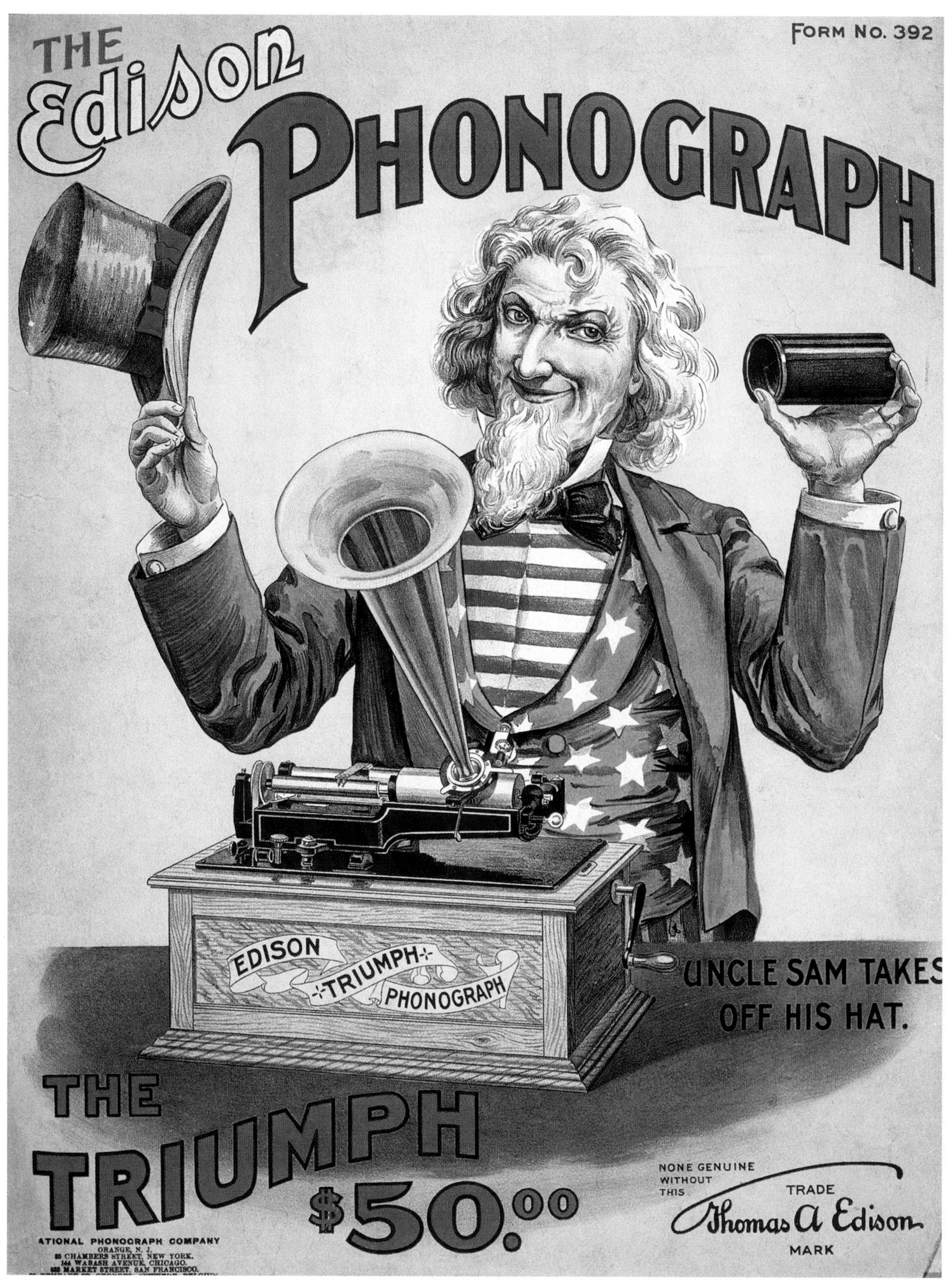
FORM NO. 392
THE Edison PHONOGRAPH
EDISON
TRIUMPH
PHONOGRAPH
UNCLE SAM TAKES OFF HIS HAT.
THE TRIUMPH
$50.00
NONE GENUINE WITHOUT THIS
TRADE
Thomas A. Edison
MARK
ATIONAL PHONOGRAPH COMPANY
ORANGE, N. J.
CHAMBERS STREET, NEW YORK.
WABASH AVENUE, CHICAGO.
MARKET STREET, SAN FRANCISCO.

Dancing is delightful
to the music of the Victrola
Every one enjoys dancing to music of such splendid volume, such clearness and perfect rhythm and the Victrola plays as long as any one wants to dance.
The Victrola brings to you all kinds of music and entertainment, superbly rendered by the world's greatest artists who make records exclusively for the Victor.
Any Victor dealer will gladly play the latest dance music or any other music you wish to hear. There are Victors and Victrolas in great variety of styles from $10 to $200.
Victor Talking Machine Co., Camden, N. J., U. S. A.
Berliner Gramophone Co., Montreal, Canadian Distributors

A left, a 1901 advertisement for a new-model Edison phonograph; above left, a Berliner gramophone, the first machine to play records; right, an ad for a later Edison competitor, the Victor Co. and its popular Victrola. Below, one of the talking dolls that Edison attempted to market in 1890.

Edison also resisted the very idea of paying royalty advances to notable artists, though in 1910 he made an exception for Sarah Bernhardt, a world-renowned actress who had won his heart when she paid a visit to his lab more than 30 years before. Worse still, for a long time he refused even to print the artists' names on the labels of records they made for him, one more reason for them not to sign with him. He tried, without success, to promote undiscovered talent among local New Jersey church choirs and choral groups. Meanwhile, he deplored all kinds of popular music as junk. Country music and vaudeville numbers made him wince. And jazz, as he once put it, was "for the nuts."

More than anything, it would be his unyielding tastes that undermined Edison's phonograph business. Few people wanted to take a gamble on a machine that could only play Edison records, when all the biggest names were recording for other labels. Although he gave the business his day-to-day attention—and perhaps because he did—by 1929 he had abandoned the whole effort. But though the phonograph had been the first idea to make him an international celebrity, by that time he had long since achieved far greater acclaim for an even more revolutionary invention—electric light.

LET THERE BE LIGHT

CHAPTER FOUR

Edison didn't discover electricity. He didn't even invent the first working light bulb. What he did was make electricity work as part of a complex system. He accomplished this by linking a more efficient dynamo to the first long-lasting incandescent bulb, and showing that it was possible to send power to hundreds of those bulbs over distances. With that, he did more than invent a glass globe. He refashioned the world.

But his discoveries were the culmination of centuries of inquiries into the nature and potential usefulness of electricity. Scientifically minded men had long been investigating this mysterious and tantalizing natural force. In his famous kite experiment of 1752, Benjamin Franklin proved that lightning was a manifestation of electricity. In 1800, the Italian physicist Alessandro Volta built the first battery that could deliver a steady charge. Made from zinc and copper disks, with brine-soaked cardboard sandwiched between

An early version of Edison's electric bulb, from 1881.

In 1879, the City of New York authorized ultrabright arc lights in locations along lower Broadway, including Madison Square, above.

them, it proved that electricity could be generated through the chemical interaction of the metals and also that it could be reliably stored—both factors crucial to its practical application.

In the early 19th century, the British chemist Sir Humphry Davy showed what a practical application might look like. In 1802, he demonstrated to the Royal Society of England the arc light, in which an arching current leaping across a small gap between carbon rods heated the rods to an intense white glow. Six years later, Davy produced the first incandescent light, whereby current was passed directly through a material—in this case a platinum wire—until it glowed.

By 1876, Paul Jablochkoff, a Russian military engineer living in Paris, had made the first practical arc lamp. But it was so bright that it was suitable only for illuminating large public spaces, and then only when mounted on tall poles so it wouldn't blind people at ground level. Compared with the warm gaslight that had been widely adopted in the mid-19th century, it was harsh and cold. "Unearthly, obnoxious to the human eye" was how the novelist Robert Louis Stevenson described the arc-lit boulevards he saw in Paris. "A lamp for a nightmare!"

Nightmare or beam into the future, in no time arc lights were being introduced into the U.S. In 1878, a Cleveland-based inventor named Charles Brush began shipping them to a few cities for use as streetlamps. Over the next several years many cities and large towns experimented with arc lighting in public places, though many would take the lights down when they found them too harsh or not as economical as promised. At the Centennial Exposition of 1876 in Philadelphia, the inventor Moses G. Farmer exhibited three variations on the arc, all powered by a dynamo—a machine that used magnetism to produce an industrial-strength electrical current—built by his collaborator William Wallace.

Wallace owned a brass and copper foundry in Ansonia, Conn., where he had built another dynamo that powered a line of eight of Farmer's outdoor arc lights. It was there, on September 8,

1878, that Thomas Edison, newly famous for inventing the phonograph the year before, had one of history's great "aha" moments.

Intrigued by the reports of Jablochkoff's arc lighting in Paris, Edison had already conducted a few offhand experiments with electric light, but none that he followed through on. Now he was paying a visit to Wallace's "light farm" at the urging of George Barker, a professor at the University of Pennsylvania who had accompanied Edison on his trip west earlier that year to view the solar eclipse. The professor believed that electricity was a field on the verge of great advances and that his brilliant young friend was just the man to usher them in.

Accompanying them that day was a reporter from the New York *Sun,* one of many who now regularly trolled in the wake of the newsworthy genius, angling for a story. And what a story he got. As the inventor was led in to see the Wallace dynamo—at that time one of the most powerful in the world—the lucky reporter preserved for posterity a description of Edison at the very moment when a world of new possibilities flooded his imagination:

> "Mr. Edison was enraptured. He fairly gloated over it. Then power was applied... and eight electric lights were kept ablaze at one time.... This filled up Mr. Edison's cup of joy. He ran from the instrument to the lights, and from the lights back to the instrument. He sprawled over a table with the simplicity of a child and made all kinds of calculations."

Wallace's dynamo convinced Edison that the problem of sending electrical current over distances had been all but solved. What remained was to invent a bulb less intense than the arc light, soft enough to use indoors. As Edison said later to the reporter from the aptly named *Sun:* "The intense light had not been subdivided." As he prepared to tear himself away from the fascinating spectacle of lights, he told Wallace: "I think I can beat you in making the electric light. I do not believe you are working in the right direction." A bemused Wallace took the bet.

Edison lost no time. If he could come up with a working electric bulb so soon after unveiling the phonograph, he almost would be, as he had predicted, producing "a big thing every six months." A day after returning to Menlo Park, he was at work on his self-assigned problem of subdivision. He felt certain that the answer lay in incandescence, not arc lighting, and that the central problem of the incandescent bulb was to find the right filament, the tiny strip of material inside the glass globe that would glow when a current was pushed through it. Within a week of his visit to the Wallace foundry he was telling the *Sun* reporter that he already had the formula for the perfect bulb. "With the process I have just discovered," he bragged, "I can produce a thousand—aye, ten thousand!" He just didn't want to make public the specifics yet.

Edison was being wildly optimistic. Or shrewdly misleading. His attorney Grosvenor P. Lowrey would soon be attempting to line up investors for his electric researches, and news of a roaring start right out of the gate wouldn't hurt. To the same reporter Edison promised that he would shortly be in a position to establish an entire electrical

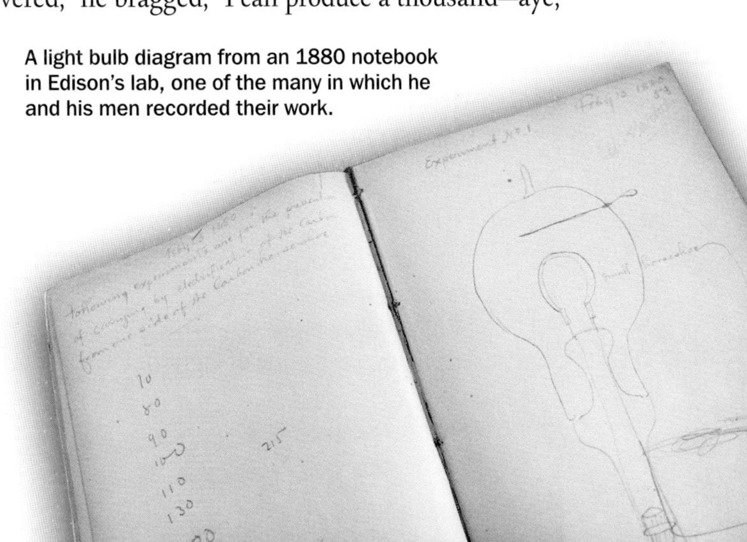

A light bulb diagram from an 1880 notebook in Edison's lab, one of the many in which he and his men recorded their work.

grid in lower Manhattan, with insulated wires running underground to bring power from central generators to customers. The share prices of gaslight companies, which would face ruinous competition if Edison's visions came true, tumbled on the news.

Lowrey established the Edison Electric Light Co., with 2,500 shares held by Edison and 500 divided among a group of investors, including the fabulously wealthy William H. Vanderbilt. This gave Edison $50,000 to fund his researches. By November, Edison was able to call in reporters individually to witness private demonstrations of his first bulb, with a platinum wire filament. The demonstrations never lasted long enough for the reporters to realize that the bulb could burn for only a few minutes before the filament gave out. Meanwhile, other inventors in the U.S. and England were rushing to bring experimental versions of the light bulb to a finished state.

With the money from his investors Edison was able to erect a large new lab at Menlo Park, stock it with costly equipment, and hire additional staff, including a German glass blower to make the bulbs. By the start of 1879, he was still issuing rosy updates to the press on his progress, but the facts were otherwise. Plainly, he needed a filament that worked better than platinum. He had also discovered the importance of producing as complete a vacuum as possible inside the glass bulb. This greatly influenced how long the filament would continue to burn but was difficult to achieve, so he had to devote part of his time, energy and staff to perfecting the vacuum process as well. As so often, Edison slept in small batches, a few hours at a time. Otherwise he was bent over his researches or wandering his lab from station to station, chewing his perennial unlit cigar.

Not content to focus on the bulb alone, Edison also embarked on the design and construction of a new, more efficient dynamo. By the spring, he and his crew had arrived at a much-improved model that they jokingly nicknamed the "long-legged Mary-Ann" because of the three-foot magnets that were part of its silhouette. But it took until autumn, with his investors nervously looking on from the sidelines, before Edison and his team finally hit upon a workable material for the filament. In October, his chief assistant, Charles Batchelor, with another staffer, spent 10 hours pumping the air out of a bulb that contained a horseshoe-shaped piece of ordinary cotton sewing thread. It had been coated in lampblack—a finely powdered black soot—and oven-baked, or "carbonized." Then the Edison lab crew switched on the bulb and checked their watches. To their great satisfaction, it burned for almost 14 hours.

Now, at last, just over a year after Edison's visit to the Wallace light farm, they were sure they were on the right track. During the next few weeks, Edison and his men would experiment with carbonized versions of all kinds of other materials, including celluloid, hemp, fishing line, and long whiskers snipped from the ample beards of two assistants. By mid-November they arrived at cardboard, which performed best of all. It burned for 170 hours. Because that was still not enough for a truly commercial bulb, his lab continued testing alternative substances, especially after it emerged that two other inventors had patents on a cardboard filament. But it was sufficient for Edison to tell the world he had found the answer.

Having held off the public and his investors for months, he quickly arranged to debut his new discovery at Menlo Park by illuminating its streets and buildings with lights strung on wires that were mounted along poles. On Dec. 27, he brought in a group of his nervous moneymen to show them he had done the thing he had boasted he could do. ("I was never myself discouraged," he recalled later. "I cannot say the same for all my associates.") Within days the outside world had gotten wind of the news. Trainloads of uninvited visitors began turning up spontaneously, eager to see the great man's latest triumph. On New Year's Eve, 3,000 of them packed Menlo Park to gape at the bright light—a foretaste of the Times Square crowds of the future. Although he made sure to keep the bulbs up and running, Edison eventually had to close off his laboratory to keep it from being overrun by curiosity seekers.

Now he threw himself into even more challenging work—developing a distribution system whereby electric power could be delivered over a wide area. From the central generators to the sockets and lamps of individual customers, this would be an immense undertaking, requiring him to conceive and develop a network of buried distributors, fuses, switches, new kinds of insulation, meters, and wiring, plus new kinds of circuitry that would keep all other bulbs lit even if one in the circuit failed or was switched off. In all, the completed system would take three years to perfect.

In April 1880, when the frozen ground of winter had thawed, Edison set to work on the first electrical grid. He had men dig narrow trenches along Menlo Park's roads and out into the surrounding fields. Into those were laid a series of long wooden boxes containing copper wire connecting Edison's generating station to a network of 400 bulbs. It was his plan to have those lights extend across an eight-mile area that would be the staging ground for another extravaganza on the following New Year's Eve.

How It Worked

Edison's incandescent bulb didn't just glow—it kept glowing.

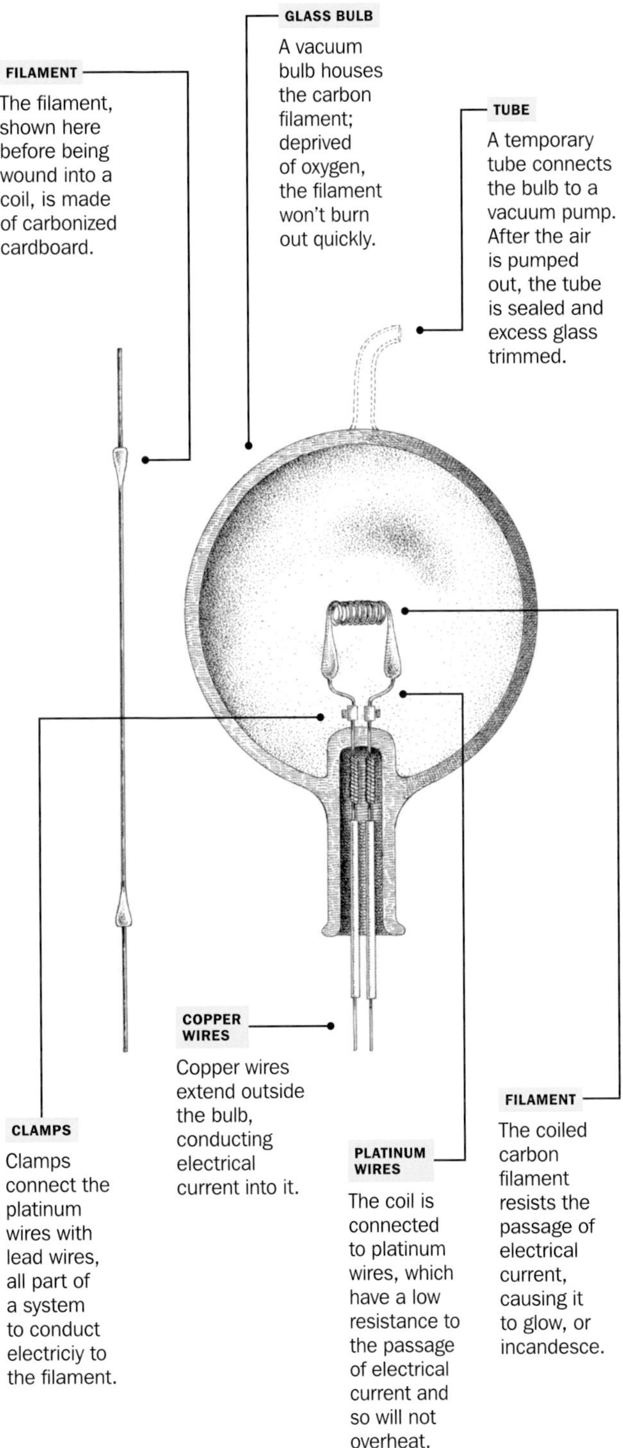

FILAMENT
The filament, shown here before being wound into a coil, is made of carbonized cardboard.
GLASS BULB
A vacuum bulb houses the carbon filament; deprived of oxygen, the filament won't burn out quickly.
TUBE
A temporary tube connects the bulb to a vacuum pump. After the air is pumped out, the tube is sealed and excess glass trimmed.
CLAMPS
Clamps connect the platinum wires with lead wires, all part of a system to conduct electriciy to the filament.
COPPER WIRES
Copper wires extend outside the bulb, conducting electrical current into it.
PLATINUM WIRES
The coil is connected to platinum wires, which have a low resistance to the passage of electrical current and so will not overheat.
FILAMENT
The coiled carbon filament resists the passage of electrical current, causing it to glow, or incandesce.

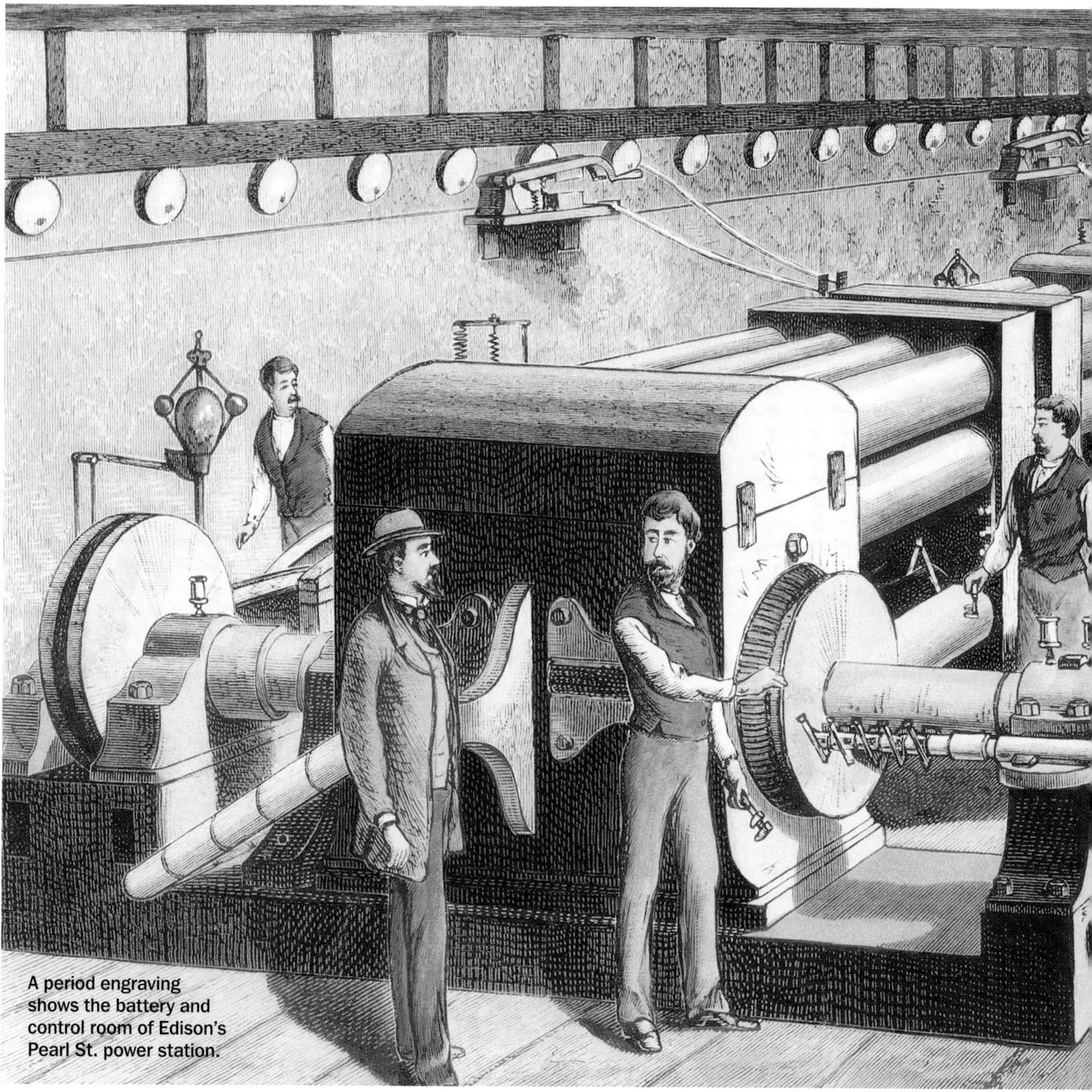

A period engraving shows the battery and control room of Edison's Pearl St. power station.

From the first, Edison wanted his wires to be buried underground like the pipes of gas companies. American cities were already being filled aboveground with a nightmare tangle of wires on poles, strung by telegraph, telephone, fire alarm, and arc lighting electric companies. These crossed streets and roofs in an ever-thickening flood of ugly and sometimes dangerous cables.

In that same month, Edison had workers lay down a half-mile of track to run an experimental electric railway in a circular route around Menlo Park. This was another innovation he was sure had a great future, and in the nearer term would be an attention-getter for the press and other visitors to his lab. But as the summer of 1880 wore on, Edison discovered that the insulation for his wires was faulty. The "subway" boxes had to be repeatedly dug up and reburied. In July, he began sending men to the far corners of the world to hunt down varieties of bamboo he thought

might serve as a replacement for cardboard in his filament. Newspapers tracked their movements. One of the men explored the Brazilian interior by canoe. Another was dispatched to Cuba, where within days he died of yellow fever. Another went to China and Japan, where he at last found a suitable specimen. This would become the filament in Edison's bulbs for most of the decade.

It was in the cities that Edison knew his future customers would be found. He had already conceived a plan for setting up his first generating plant in lower Manhattan, from which he would extend wires to power the immediate neighborhood—a demonstration model far more impressive than any mere New Year's light show at Menlo Park. He knew there was no time to lose. A rival company, using a bulb that Edison felt was plainly copied from his design, had soon established its own Manhattan base and was selling electrical systems with on-site generators to businesses and post offices. And by the end of the year, the arc light inventor/ entrepreneur Charles Brush had persuaded the city to allow him to set up a trial display of his ultrabright light poles along lower Broadway.

By the spring of 1881, Menlo Park was no longer Edison's base of operations. The previous December, he had obtained with great difficulty the consent of New York's famously corrupt city government to build his proposed network on the southern tip of Manhattan. (He got their approval in part by plying them with a lavish champagne dinner at Menlo Park catered by Delmonico's, then New York's finest restaurant.) With his attention increasingly focused on that project, he found a building on lower Fifth Ave. to serve as a new headquarters and moved with his family to a hotel nearby. Soon he was supervising the installation of his underground wires, all 14 miles of them. He formed companies to make lamp bulbs, electrical fixtures, and the all-important dynamos in factories around Manhattan. He bought two buildings on Pearl St. to house his generating plant. By July, the first enormous dynamo, custom built by him, was installed.

But not until Sept. 4, 1882, was Edison finally ready. At three o'clock on that day, John Lieb, an engineer at the Pearl St. station, threw a switch. A few blocks away, in the Wall Street offices of J.P. Morgan, members of Edison's electric company were gathered. Edison threw another switch. Inside the office, the lights came on, as they did in 300 bulbs in other offices around the neighborhood. Those included the headquarters of the New York *Times*, which reported favorably to its readers on the brightness and steadiness of the new electric light. Edison had done it.

By now, Edison was as much a businessman as an inventor, shepherding the electrical power industry into existence. Even before the success of Pearl St., his company had built numerous on-site power systems for individual businesses, private mansions, and even a large ship. It had put on spectacular displays of lighting at the International Electrical Exhibition in Paris in 1881 and at

Edison wed Mina Miller, above, in 1886, 18 months after the death of his first wife. Educated and self-possessed, Mina took an interest in his work and even briefly helped to record the results of lab experiments. Together they had three children, from left, Theodore, Charles, and Madeleine.

·−− ·· ·−·· ·−··/−·−− −−− ··−/−− ·− ·−· ·−· −·−−/−− · ?

−·−− · ··· .

[Edison proposed to Mina Miller in Morse code. He tapped out: "Will you marry me?" She answered: "Yes."]

London's Crystal Palace Exhibition the following year, where it also introduced the first electrical sign—spelling out Edison's name in lights. His chief assistant, Batchelor, was overseeing Edison operations all over Europe. And now that he had succeeded in New York, other American cities, including Boston, Chicago, and Detroit, were ready to gamble on Edison systems of their own. But they would spread more slowly at first than he hoped, in part because they required large capital outlays to build generating plants and lay wires.

While Edison's business was flourishing, his personal life was suddenly in upheaval. Throughout their marriage, his wife, Mary, had frequently been in poor health, suffering headaches, fatigue, and panic attacks. But in July 1884, she became much more seriously ill, perhaps from typhoid fever, as her daughter Marion later recalled. On Aug. 9, she died, just 29 years old. Obsessed with work, Edison had never been devoted to home life. But he was shaken by his wife's death. Years later, Marion still remembered her father waking her on the morning after her mother's death, "shaking with grief, weeping, and sobbing."

Glenmont, the home that Edison bought in January 1886, just before his marriage to his second wife, Mina.

Mary's death left Edison, at 37, a widower with three children in his care. Marion was an 11 year-old attending school in New York. For a time, the boys were sent back to Menlo Park to live with Mary's relatives. Edison would need a new wife, and in short order he was looking for one, with the help of his good friend Ezra Gilliland and his wife. They invited Edison frequently to their home in Boston, where they made sure also to invite a succession of eligible young women. One of them was 19-year-old Mina Miller. The dark-eyed daughter of a wealthy Ohio farm equipment manufacturer, she was studying music at a women's seminary in Boston. Edison soon found himself captivated by her beauty, intelligence, and self-possession. He taught her Morse code, so that they could communicate privately by tapping on their own hands even when they were in the company of others. In the early autumn of 1885, on a trip to New Hampshire with the Gillilands, he dared to tap out the words "Will you marry me?" She tapped back: "Yes."

They were married the following February at the Miller family home in Akron, Ohio. Even before the ceremony, they had picked out a new house for themselves. Grander than anything Edison had previously occupied, "Glenmont" was a 29-room, Queen Anne-style red brick mansion. It sat on about 13 acres in Llewellyn Park, the first planned suburb in America, located in West

Edison's West Orange laboratory is now a National Historic Site. At left, the interior of one of its primary workspaces. Above, the arched entrance and the main building.

Orange, N.J. It boasted stained glass windows, spacious rooms, and stables. Before his new marriage, Edison still lived to some extent like the country boy he had been, a man of simple tastes and slightly threadbare wardrobe. Mina would see to it that he lived in a way more in keeping with his increasing wealth. Although Edison was suspicious of formal education, having had almost none of it himself, she saw to it that his sons went to the best boarding schools to prepare them for the best colleges. She helped oversee plans for the new winter home they were building in Fort Myers, Fla. She also had a better grasp of his work than his first wife, and even briefly assisted in recording the results of experiments in his laboratory.

The final piece of Edison's new life was the immense lab and workshop he set out to build in West Orange. By the summer of 1887, it was going up on 14 acres near his home. The principal building, a three-story brick structure with tall arched windows, was designed by the same architect who had produced Edison's house, though the two men would have a falling out before work on the project was completed. It contained a heavy-machine shop filled with the best equipment, another for lighter precision machinery, a large lab, and a multistory library/office for Edison with an alcove for the bed he used for catnaps. He also provided himself with his own private experimental chamber. Four additional buildings would be erected nearby for chemical and electrical research.

The West Orange complex was more than just a laboratory. It was a personal fiefdom for an inventor who was also by now a rising industrialist, and it was ready just in time for Edison to face one of the greatest challenges of his life as a businessman. Real competition for electrical customers was appearing, and not just from familiar parties like the arc light entrepreneur Brush. A new company, Thomson-Houston, was manufacturing incandescent lights using a model that Edison felt was clearly an infringement of his patented design. More ominously, the aggressive young industrialist George Westinghouse was doing the same. By 1885, Edison was locked in lawsuits against both companies that would drag on for seven years. But the true danger to Edison's dominance of the electrical market lay in the effort by Westinghouse to market a form of electrical power fundamentally different from the "direct current" offered by Edison. Because it could travel over wires for considerable distances without losing strength, something direct current could not do, the "alternating current" promoted by Westinghouse had considerable appeal, especially to municipalities planning to set up electrical systems to service far-flung neighborhoods and looking to avoid the multiple power stations that Edison's short-range systems required. As a consequence, Edison was soon locked in a years-long public relations war with Westinghouse over the virtues of their respective systems. The "war of the currents," pitting alternating current against direct current—AC vs. DC—was about to begin.

HOW EDISON LOST THE RACE TO ELECTRIFY AMERICA

By Jill Jonnes

To Thomas Edison and his Wall Street backers, his success in perfecting the incandescent bulb and building an electrical grid in lower Manhattan was but the beginning of what they hoped would become a lucrative empire of light and power. Edison's innovations would not only light the world, they would drive factory engines to power the ever-expanding realms of industry.

But no sooner had he unveiled his new bulbs and generators than competitors were lining up. The most formidable was the Pittsburgh industrialist George Westinghouse, a man roughly Edison's age who had invented the railway airbrake. Westinghouse took a serious interest in electricity around 1885, but not in Edison's low-voltage, direct-current (DC) system. He doubted the longer-term prospects for direct current for the simple reason that DC-generating plants could not transmit electricity economically for more than half a mile. Alternating current systems could send power much farther, meaning for one thing that cities could use fewer central power stations to serve their populations.

While Edison preferred his companies to use technologies he had invented or perfected himself, Westinghouse had no such compunctions. In 1885, he snapped up the patents for a radical new European technology. It used alternating current (AC) to send high-voltage electricity over great distances, before stepping down the power with transformers to make it safe for customer use. By the end of the following year, having formed the Westinghouse Electric Co., he was already showcasing his new system at an upscale department store in Buffalo.

But AC had its problems, too. Handled improperly, its high voltage carried the risk of serious shocks, a risk that Edison was ready to point to over and over again in what would become an increasingly fraught struggle to define

At left, New York's lower Broadway in 1880, with its overhead tangle of telephone and telegraph wires. Edison insisted on burying the wires for his Pearl St. electrical grid. At top, George Westinghouse, who would pit alternating current against Edison's direct current. Above, Nikola Tesla failed to interest Edison in the idea of his AC motor.

AC in the public mind. He wrote darkly to one of his top executives: "Westinghouse will kill a customer within six months after he puts in a system of any size." Edison's DC systems had an additional advantage. They could be used to run motors; alternating current could not. In effect, its continual change of direction confused them. Until someone found a way to solve that problem, AC would have only limited applications for industry.

Someone who thought he might find an answer was Nikola Tesla, one of the world's true eccentric geniuses. A Serb from Croatia,

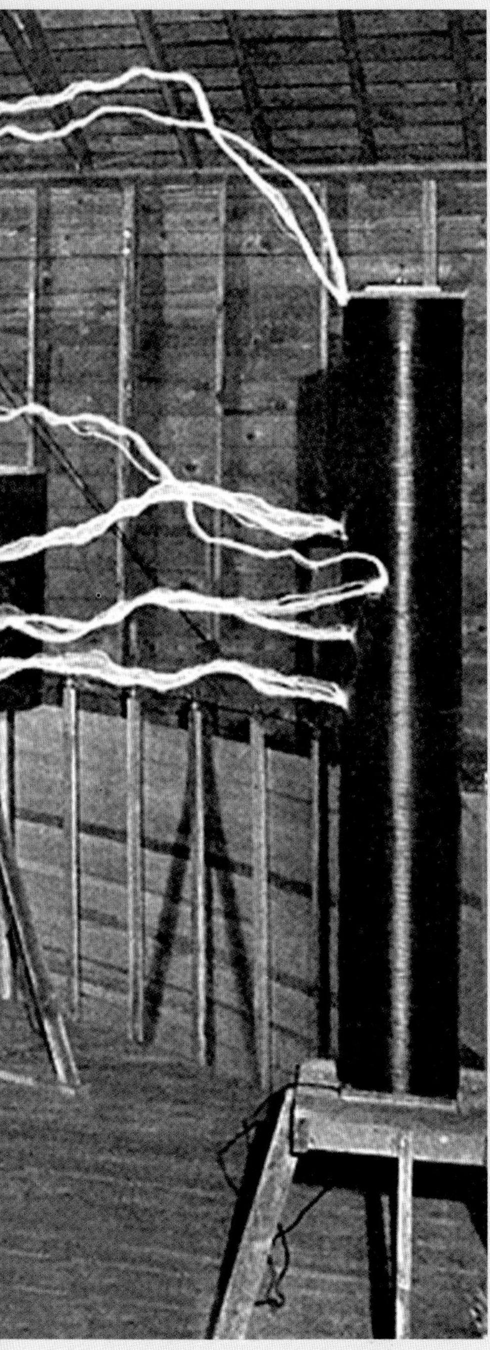

At left, a double-exposure photo from around 1899 shows Tesla in the Colorado lab where he spent years exploring high-voltage electricity. Above, the grisly electrocution in 1889 of telegraph lineman John Feeks heightened fears about alternating current.

born in 1856, Tesla first became fascinated by electricity as a child, when he discovered that by petting his cat he could produce sparks. Looking back years later, he recalled asking himself: "Is nature a giant cat? Who strokes its back?"

As a young man, Tesla went on to study electrical engineering in Graz, Austria, and then in Prague, until his father's death compelled him to drop out of school and take a job with the phone company in Budapest. There, overwork led him to suffer a nervous breakdown. During his recuperation, while on a sunset stroll in a city park, he had an almost mystical vision of an AC motor design. Gripped with excitement, he snapped a large twig from a nearby tree and scratched out the motor's outlines in the ground for the amazed friend who was with him that day. "Isn't it beautiful?" he cried out. "Now I can die happy. But I must live. I must return to work and build the motor so I can give it to the world."

That was in February 1882. Two years later, after

The 5,000-horsepower generators made by Westinghouse for the Niagara Falls Power Co. The Niagara project was a milestone in the spread of alternating current.

a stint in the Paris offices of Edison's increasingly trans-Atlantic company, Tesla was in New York, working directly for the great man himself and hoping to bring him into the AC fold. But Edison wouldn't hear of it, telling Tesla there was no future in "deadly" AC. Then Tesla was denied a big bonus he thought he had been promised. He left Edison's New York office and soon formed his own arc lighting company, hoping to develop his AC motor independently.

By late 1887, the Westinghouse Electric & Manufacturing Co. had become the biggest competitor of Edison General Electric. Edison had built or begun 121 DC stations in various parts of the U.S. For Westinghouse, the number of AC stations was 68 and climbing. The appeal of AC, with its longer-range capabilities, was growing, especially for smaller cities whose most prosperous citizens — the ones most able to pay for electricity at home — tended to live in outlying suburbs.

Pressed on all sides by top associates, Edison reluctantly acquired patents for a European AC system that he hesitated to actually produce, especially while he was launching ever more bitter attacks against Westinghouse and the presumed dangers of alternating current. It was a campaign assisted every time the newspapers reported that a faulty or severed wire had electrocuted a lineman. Edison also cooperated in a successful effort to ensure that Westinghouse current would be used for the first electric chair. He hoped this would cement an association in the public mind between AC and death by electricity. (See next page.)

The competition between the two men became more heated after Tesla, who had been cheated by his partners in the arc lighting business and was reduced at one point to digging ditches, at last unveiled his AC motor in 1888. It worked beautifully. Duly impressed, Westinghouse lost no time in buying Tesla's patents and hiring him to engineer a commercial version of his miraculous engine. If AC could finally run motors, its victory in the "War of the Electric Currents" was assured.

Over the next several years, there were rumors of a possible merger between Edison General Electric and another rival, the Thomson-Houston Electric Co. Edison always dismissed this talk, but the matter was not truly in his hands as long as the bulk of his company's shares were controlled by the financier J. P. Morgan. The immensely wealthy and powerful Morgan had been an early supporter of Edison. In 1882, not long after becoming an investor in his first electric company, Morgan even had Edison install a private generator and lighting system at his mansion on Madison Ave. He had given Edison systems as gifts to a school and a church, and had talked up his home system to wealthy friends, who put in orders for their own. But in business matters, Morgan was entirely unsentimental, as Edison would learn to his regret.

On Feb. 5, 1892, Alfred O. Tate, Edison's personal secretary, was at his desk at company headquarters in lower Manhattan when a reporter came by to tell him that Morgan was about to announce the merger of Edison's company with Thomson-Houston— a development Edison knew nothing about. Because Thomson-Houston's president, Charles Coffin, had shown Morgan that his firm was earning almost twice the profits of Edison's, Morgan had also decided that Coffin would run the merged operation. Worse, he erased Edison's name. The new company would be called, simply, General Electric.

In the years that followed, the growth of AC systems would continue to outpace direct current. A milestone for Westinghouse was winning the contract for what would be a highly publicized project to build a vast hydro-electric plant at Niagara Falls that would supply the city of Buffalo. It was completed in 1895. Although his company expanded and prospered mightily over the next decade, in the financial panic of 1907 it went bankrupt. Even after it emerged from bankruptcy a few years later, Westinghouse, like Edison, was shoved aside by his moneymen.

As for Edison, after the surprise merger with Thomson-Houston, he had little further involvement in the development of electrical power. Following the merger, he expressed some bitterness to Tate on his whole long involvement with electricity. "I've come to the conclusion I never did know anything about it," he said, vowing to do something "so different and so much bigger...people will forget that my name was ever connected with anything electrical."

Of course, nothing of the sort happened. He went on to do, as promised, many different things. But none that would make the world forget that it was his genius that launched the electrical revolution.

Jonnes is the author of Empires of Light: Edison, Tesla, Westinghouse, and the Race to Electrify the World. *This is a revised and expanded version of a piece that first appeared in* Time.

SERIOUS CHARGES: EDISON, WESTINGHOUSE & THE ELECTRIC CHAIR

By Richard Moran

On Aug. 6, 1890, William Kemmler, a peddler from Buffalo who had murdered his mistress with an ax, became the first man to die in the electric chair. At 6:40 a.m., in the death chamber of Auburn state prison, Kemmler was administered two applications of electricity. The first, 1,300 volts, lasted for only 17 seconds and proved insufficient to kill him. The second charge was 2,000 volts. After four minutes, the smell of burning flesh filled the room as the condemned man caught fire. As soon as his charred body stopped smoldering, Kemmler was pronounced dead.

The Kemmler execution was not only a grisly milestone in the history of capital punishment; it was a notable episode in a public relations war—the battle of the electric currents—between Thomas Edison and his archrival, George Westinghouse. What was at stake was the public perception of alternating current (AC), the system promoted by Westinghouse in a fierce competition with Edison's direct current (DC). Almost from the moment he introduced AC in 1886, four years after Edison unveiled DC, Westinghouse began to cut seriously into Edison's market share. So by 1888, Edison and his supporters had launched a campaign to convince the public of the dangers of AC, which operated at much higher voltages. Because AC dynamos manufactured by Westinghouse were the method chosen to supply the lethal current for the chair—despite the best efforts of Westinghouse to prevent it—the Kemmler execution became an opportunity for Edison to identify AC in the public mind as "the executioner's current."

The grotesque reality of the Kemmler execution notwithstanding, the electric chair was devised as a means of making capital punishment more acceptable to the American public. In the late 1880s, after several highly publicized hangings that were gruesomely bungled, support for the death penalty had begun to wane. Its defenders felt compelled to go in search of a more reliable and less painful method of execution. In 1887, Dr. Alfred Southwick, a member of a commission established by the New York State Legislature to explore alternatives, including electrocution and lethal injection, contacted Edison by mail to seek his recommendations. At first the great man refused—he was, after all, an opponent of capital punishment. But when Southwick went to him again, Edison realized that this could be an opportunity. He suggested that the "best appliance" to kill "instantaneously" and with the "least amount of suffering" was an AC dynamo "manufactured principally... by George Westinghouse."

On June 4, 1888, New York State legalized death by electricity, though without specifying what kind of current should be used. The

Kemmler, the first man to die in the electric chair, at his execution.

following day, Harold Brown, a self-taught New York City engineer, inserted himself into the crusade against AC. He wrote a letter to the *New York Evening Post* outlining the dangers of AC and accusing Westinghouse of placing his financial interests ahead of the public welfare. Brown then teamed up with Edison. At Edison's West Orange, N.J., laboratory, he conducted experiments demonstrating that less than 300 volts of AC would kill a dog that had survived 1,000 volts of DC. Later, before a New York City audience of "electricians" and journalists, Brown electrocuted a 76-lb. dog named Dash. Afterward, he proclaimed that alternating current was suitable only for "the dog pound, the slaughterhouse, and the state prison."

One year later, the ax murderer Kemmler was sentenced to death by electrocution. Lawyers paid for by Westinghouse appealed the sentence to the New York State Supreme Court, claiming that electrocution was cruel and unusual punishment. Before an evidentiary hearing held to assess the issues raised by Kemmler's attorneys, Edison assured the court that death by alternating current was quick and painless. Predictably, Kemmler's motion was denied, as was a similar petition to the U.S. Supreme Court.

Despite the prominence of Brown's attacks on AC, the New York State superintendent of prisons hired Brown to design and install the first electric chair. With Brown building it, of course it would be an AC chair. As expected, Westinghouse refused to sell Brown his powerful AC generators. But with Edison working behind the scenes, Brown secured three through a secondhand dealer in Boston.

In the end, the controversies surrounding Kemmler's execution did not damage Westinghouse's business. Within a year, AC had captured 50% of the lighting market. In 1893, when Westinghouse Electric signed a contract to install AC generators at Niagara Falls, the battle of the electrical currents had been won—and not by Edison.

Richard Moran is the author of Executioner's Current: Thomas Edison, George Westinghouse, and the Invention of the Electric Chair.

BRIGHT LIGHTS, BIG CITIES

Americans loved the new electric light, and in the decades after Edison introduced the incandescent bulb they found ever more imaginative and extravagant ways to display it—though the power for their glittering spectacles was often supplied by his competitors.

Luna Park, one of the great amusement arcades at New York's Coney Island, around 1900. For its many thousands of annual visitors, the blazing lights created a safe but exciting enclave in the night.

HUMAN
DYNAMO
AERIAL NIGHT ATTACKS

3

The Electric Tower, at far left, was one of the centerpieces of the 1901 Pan-American Exposition in Buffalo, a showcase for the power of electricity that drew current from the Westinghouse hydroelectric plant at Niagara Falls. At top, New York's Times Square in the 1920s, already a great cluster of electric signage; above, Seattle's Bon Marché department store in 1902; to light the World's Columbian Exposition in Chicago in 1893, at left, the Westinghouse company installed hundreds of generators and 250,000 bulbs.

LIGHTS, CAMERA, EDISON

CHAPTER FIVE

By the autumn of 1888, Edison may have been the busiest man in America. Working in his splendid new laboratory in West Orange, he was absorbed in perfecting his phonograph, testing improved filaments for his light bulb, and overseeing the spread of Edison electrical systems around the U.S. At the same time, he was working on a project that would consume him for years to come. It involved the use of magnetic power to separate iron ore from the rock or sand in which it was embedded. Amid all this, he and Mina had somehow also found the time that spring to welcome a daughter, Madeleine, the first of three children they would have together.

Just a year into his 40s, Edison was unflaggingly energetic and his questing mind still keen for the next thing. Soon the next thing presented itself. Having invented a machine that recorded sound, could he make one that recorded motion?

Edison examines film for his Home Kinetoscope, a projector he introduced in 1911. It was a short-lived precursor to later home movie equipment.

By the late 19th century, that question was much in the air—literally. In the 1870s, the photographer Eadweard Muybridge began experimenting with stop-action photography to study animal movement. By placing a long line of glass plate cameras along a race track, each of them triggered in sequence as a horse trotted past, he made stop-action pictures proving that horses at full gallop repeatedly lift all four hooves off the ground at the same time. In the next decade, Muybridge examined the action of men leaping and wrestling, women walking and gesturing, and birds in flight. Some of these photographs he used as the basis for sequential drawings painted on the surface of a revolving glass disk. When the disk was spun with a light directed through it, the rapid sequence of drawings produced the illusion of movement. He called his optical device a "zoopraxiscope." In February 1888, after demonstrating the device for a lecture audience in West Orange, he paid a call on Edison to discuss the possibility of combining his moving images with Edison's recorded sound.

Edison was intrigued, though not enough to go into partnership with Muybridge. He probably realized the impracticality of a system requiring multiple cameras. But what about a single camera that could take multiple pictures? In October, after receiving from Muybridge a full set of his photographs, Edison filed a "patent caveat"—an early announcement of a pending invention, but without technical details—that described his thinking this way:

> "I am experimenting with an instrument which does for the eye what the phonograph does for the ear, which is the recording and reproduction of things in motion, and in such a form as to be both cheap, practical, and convenient. This apparatus I call a kinetoscope, "moving view"...

As he went on to explain, Edison envisioned a camera that would make a series of tiny sequential photographs "in a continuous spiral on a cylinder," not unlike the cylinders his phonographs used to record sound. After each exposure, the cylinder would halt for a fraction of a second, then advance at high speed for the next. Very high speed—Edison initially expected a stop-and-go rate of 40 pictures per second. To oversee the project, he assigned one of his assistants, William Kennedy Laurie Dickson, who though immersed in the ore-milling experiments was also a photographer. Dickson would do much of the actual work to develop the camera. He and Edison gave the new effort what time they could spare from their other pursuits.

In the coming months, as he tried out ways to make sequential pictures inside a single box, Dickson tested out various photographic emulsions applied to spinning cylinders. Before long, he

Stop-action photos made by Eadweard Muybridge in the 1870s proved that horses at full gallop lift all four hooves off the ground at once.

arrived at a device in which big sheets of a new product called celluloid were wrapped around an aluminum drum. But by the spring of 1889, it was obvious that a swiftly rotating cylinder was too cumbersome to be practical. In August, Edison departed for Europe to attend the Paris Exposition, leaving Dickson to move forward on the camera. In Paris he made the acquaintance of Étienne-Jules Marey, a Frenchman who, like Muybridge, had been fascinated by sequential photography and had developed a camera that made 60 images per second on a strip of film. Dickson might also have known of Marey's work from published sources. Certainly by the time Edison returned to West Orange in October, Dickson had made remarkable progress on his own, even to the extent of rigging up a system that projected images on a screen that were synced with recorded sound. When the inventor returned from France, he was welcomed by a film in which Dickson appeared, tipped his hat, and said, "Good morning, Mr. Edison. Glad to see you back. I hope you are satisfied with the kineto-phonograph."

But Edison wasn't ready yet to take interest in a projection system, much less sound, not when the camera was still unfinished business. Having decided to abandon the cylinder model, he and Dickson chose to cut the sheets of transparent celluloid into strips, narrow ribbons that could speed past the camera's shutter. (Eventually they would discover George Eastman's new film stock.) The strips of celluloid would have sprockets running along each side, allowing them to be ratcheted forward by the motorized cogwheels of the camera. In their brick workshop in New Jersey, Edison and Dickson were a continent away from the Los Angeles neighborhood that would later become famous as Hollywood, but in their first spooling ribbons of celluloid, motion picture film was being born. And with it, the movies.

Like a still camera, Edison's "kinetograph," as he called it, produced a negative from which a positive image could be developed. It still remained for him to create a device for watching the movie that resulted. His solution to that problem would be the kinetoscope. In the early 1890s, he was discovering the profitability of coin-operated phonographs in public arcades. His kinetoscope was designed with the same possibilities in mind. It was housed in a wooden cabinet about four feet high. To watch a short film, the viewer bent over the cabinet and looked through an eyepiece and lens located at the top. Inside was battery-powered machinery that ran a 50-foot strip of film along a bank of spools and past the lens, where a high-speed shutter paused each still frame before the viewer for the tiniest fraction of a second. The phenomenon known as persistence of vision caused the brain to register the series of still images as continuous movement.

The Black Maria, Edison's studio on wheels, was mounted on a revolving pivot so that it could be rotated on a circular track to follow the daily movement of the sun across the sky.

Edison debuted his peephole kinetoscope in May 1891 before a convention of the National Federation of Women's Clubs. By the time he filed a patent for it in August, he had decided that the width of the film it used should be 35 millimeters, the dimension that would become the industry standard for moviemaking. It was an industry he would soon find himself doing a great deal to create. Edison wasn't the first person to recognize that moving pictures had a future as a form of entertainment. The Muybridge zoopraxiscope was only one of several projection devices that proved their power to amuse audiences in the late 19th century. But after an initial reluctance to grasp its real money-making potential—the same mistake he had made with the phonograph—Edison eventually understood film's ability to fascinate people. At the same time, he also opened the way for other entrepreneurs to create what would become the moviegoing public.

As late as February 1894, Edison could write to Muybridge that he had produced 25 coin-in-slot machines, while adding, "I am very doubtful there is any commercial feature in it and fear that they will not earn their cost." But his secretary, Alfred O. Tate, thought otherwise. Tate and his brother were among the investors in the first kinetoscope parlor, which opened in April on lower Broadway. Because none of their 10 machines were able to accept coins, they charged 25 cents for a ticket that allowed a customer to watch five films. On opening day, they were mobbed. In his book *The Wizard of Menlo Park*, a shrewd portrait of Edison's career as a public figure, Randall Stross writes: "They could not get the place cleared before 1 a.m. on Sunday....Without advertising they had taken in $120 on the first day."

Other parlors followed, fueling demand for kinetoscopes and turning them into a very "commercial" business indeed. Even before the first arcade debuted, Edison had set up a primitive filmmaking operation in West Orange. The centerpiece was a strangely shaped wooden studio building completed in February 1893. He and his men called it the Black Maria, after the police paddy wagons it somewhat resembled. An eccentric structure covered with black tarpaper—"it obeys no architectural rules," Dickson explained—it had a room jutting from one end with a hinged roof that could be raised or lowered to control the amount of natural light. The entire building was mounted on a revolving pivot and wheels that made it possible to turn it to catch the sun as it moved across the sky.

In his unexpected role as one of America's first filmmakers, Dickson invited all kinds of people to the Black Maria to do something, anything, before the camera that might sustain interest for the 20 seconds or so that the first films ran. For the earliest copyrighted film, from January 7, 1894, Edison's assistant Fred Ott simply performed a comic sneeze. The famous strongman Eugen Sandow agreed to flex for the camera for $250, then declined the money if he could just shake Edison's hand. Vaudeville troupers, knife throwers, and chorus girls appeared. Performers from Buffalo Bill's Wild West Show came by, including Annie Oakley.

As it turned out, boxing matches staged at the studio were among the most popular subjects. Two brothers, Grey and Otway Latham, working with their friend Enoch Rector, persuaded Edison to film fights in the Black Maria that they could exhibit in the Manhattan kinetoscope parlor they opened in the summer of 1896. Rector worked with Edison's lab to adapt Edison's camera and kinetoscope to produce and show one-minute films. That was long enough to hold an entire abbreviated round of a six-round battle, allowing the brothers to charge customers separately to see each one. When their first filmed bout proved a big hit, they recruited

Trick of the Eye

To make pictures that moved, Edison's camera shot a rapid sequence of stills.

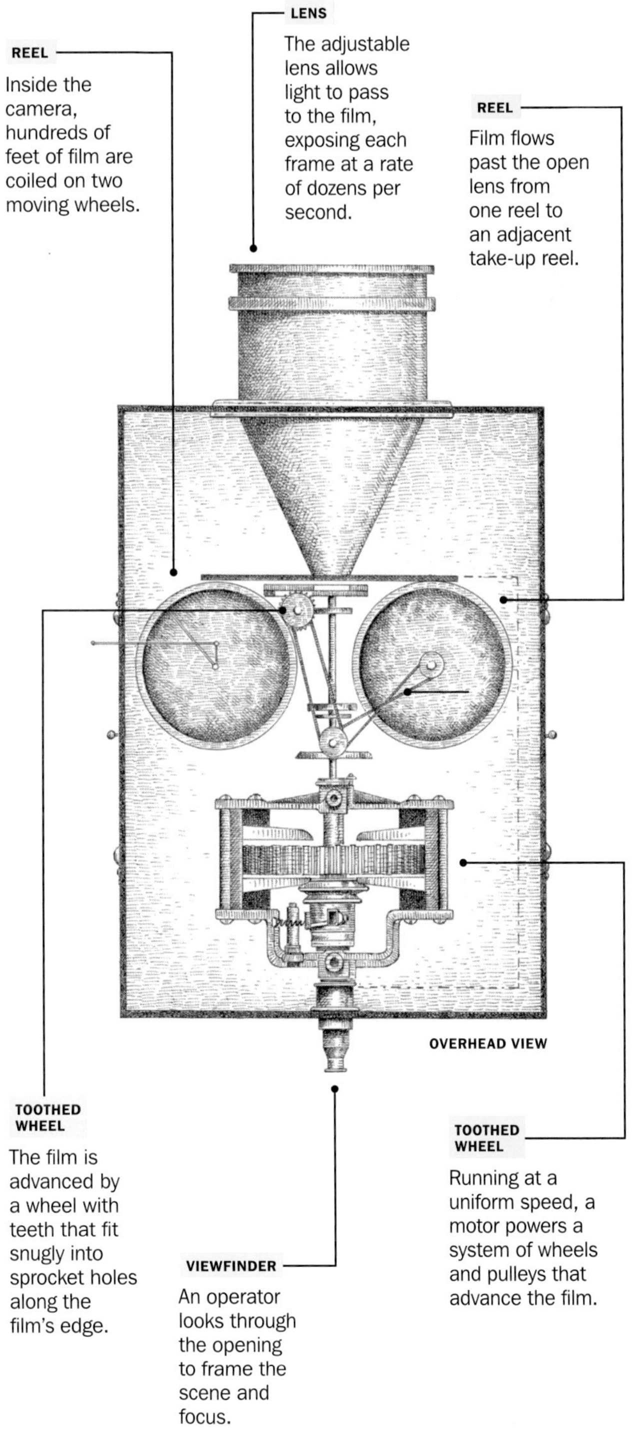

LENS
The adjustable lens allows light to pass to the film, exposing each frame at a rate of dozens per second.
REEL
Inside the camera, hundreds of feet of film are coiled on two moving wheels.
REEL
Film flows past the open lens from one reel to an adjacent take-up reel.
OVERHEAD VIEW
TOOTHED WHEEL
The film is advanced by a wheel with teeth that fit snugly into sprocket holes along the film's edge.
VIEWFINDER
An operator looks through the opening to frame the scene and focus.
TOOTHED WHEEL
Running at a uniform speed, a motor powers a system of wheels and pulleys that advance the film.

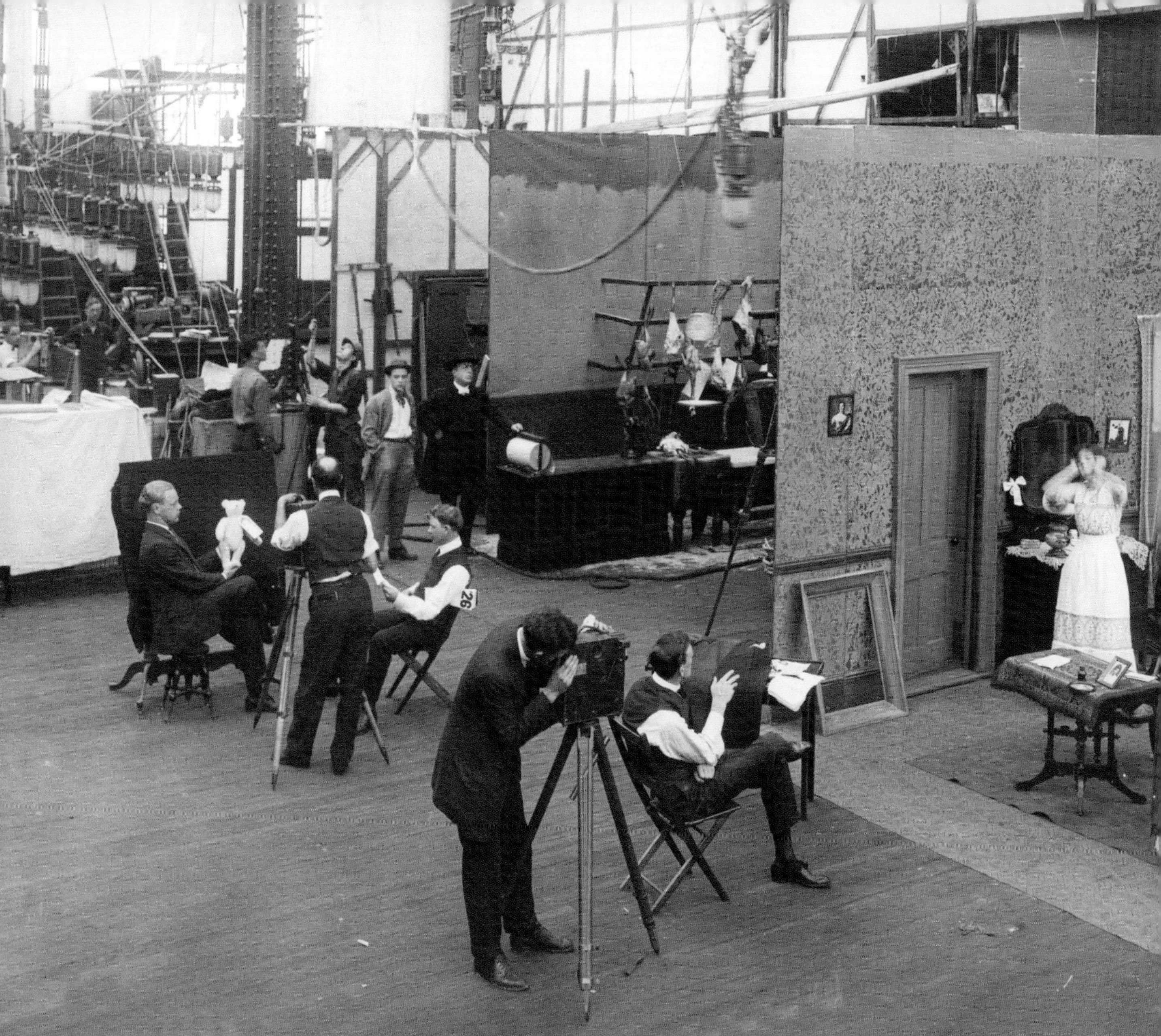

Directors, cameramen, and performers at work on the set at Edison's glass-enclosed film studio in the Bronx.

for their next the popular prizefighter "Gentleman Jim" Corbett. Fearing that Corbett would make quick work of any opponent—too quick to ensure a fight long enough for six films—their contract with him stipulated that he should knock out the other man no sooner than the sixth round. He easily complied. Although the Black Maria was well lit, it was apparently poorly ventilated. Corbett insisted years later that "the little movable studio was the hottest, most cramped place I have ever known."

The Lathams quickly realized something Edison still refused to see—that films would be even more profitable when they could be projected on a screen before large paying audiences. Edison worried that theatrical presentation would cut into the profits for his kinetoscopes and wanted no part of any effort to develop the necessary projectors. The Lathams took it upon themselves to make the attempt, getting advice from none other than Dickson, who eventually left Edison to work for them. By April 1895, they had a working model and just a month later were able to exhibit on a movie screen a boxing match they had filmed on the roof of Madison Square Garden. But images produced by the Lathams' projector weren't truly clear. There was room for a superior projector. Soon a pair of inventors in Washington, D.C., were working on the problem. In September, Thomas Armat and C. Francis Jenkins unveiled a projector that stopped each frame of film in front of the projector lamp for a split second before advancing to the next, which had the effect of producing a bright, clear image. But soon after, they dissolved their partnership.

By that time, Edison had already promised reporters that he would be producing his own projector, though in fact he was so preoccupied by his faltering ore-extracting business that he did nothing. The largest distributor of his kinetoscopes, Raff & Gammon, was anxious to convert to a projector system. When Armat gave the business partners an impressive demonstration of his machine, they came up with a plan. They got both him and Edison to agree that Edison would market Armat's device under his name. In April 1896, the Armat projector, now called the Vitascope and distributed as an Edison product, debuted at a New York music hall. The program of short films included ballerinas, boxers, and crashing waves. An audience full of celebrities from the theater and business worlds greeted the dawn of true motion pictures with a cheer.

Above, a customer views a film through the eyepiece of an Edison kinetoscope. At right, the console of a kinetoscope opened to display its interior mechanism and its looping belt of 35mm film.

In the following year, Edison finally introduced a projector of his own design. Soon he would build a sizable new studio in the Bronx, N.Y., and his filmmaking operation would take on a closer resemblance to what we think of as a Hollywood movie factory. His most imaginative directors began turning out films with story lines like *The Life of an American Fireman*, from 1903, and *The Great Train Robbery*, a 12-minute hit Western made the following year. Both were by Edwin S. Porter. All around the U.S. there was an explosion of movie houses, known as "nickelodeons" because they charged 5 cents for admission to see a variety of 10-to-15-minute "story films," as well as travelogues, sporting events, and music and comedy acts.

Edison never devoted much of his own time to overseeing his movie operations, even as they, along with his phonograph companies, became a significant source of profits, helping him in the 1890s to absorb the substantial losses from his ore-milling schemes. It's one of the great ironies of Edison's life story that popular culture was never a comfort zone for him, even as we remember him as the man who gave us the machinery that made so much of it possible.

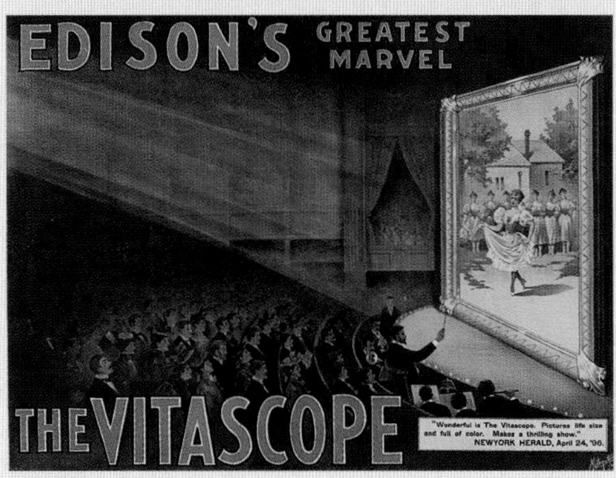

KISS, KISS, BANG, BANG! BIRTH OF A MOVIE NATION

By Richard Corliss

Toward the end of MGM's 1940 biopic *Edison, the Man*, starring Spencer Tracy, an honor roll of Thomas Edison's achievements marches onto the screen: Fluoroscope! Mimeograph! Storage battery! And then to the heart of the matter for the film industry: Motion pictures! Projection machine! Talking pictures! In its golden age, Hollywood was paying tribute to the man who, nearly a half-century earlier, possessed the genius and foresight to invent the movies.

It wasn't that simple a story. The movies love a lone hero, and Edison was a natural for Hollywood hagiography. But the birth of movies had many obstetricians. Étienne-Jules Marey and the Lumière brothers in France, William Friese-Greene in Britain, Eadweard Muybridge in the U.S.—these and others contributed to the "invention" of movies. So did some of Edison's employees, who were obscured by their boss's starlight.

Edison's movies include some of the best-known titles in early cinema, among them

The Kiss, Fatima's Dance, and *The Great Train Robbery*. Experimenting with sound, color, and special effects in a variety of genres, they are the clear ancestors of the next century of films.

Historians still debate the extent of the founder's participation in the process. What's unquestioned is Edison's erroneous belief that the future of movies lay in his peepshow kinetoscope, which allowed only one viewer at a time, rather than in images projected on a screen before a large audience. Edison's 19th-century toy, showing short films of watermelon-eating contests and cats with boxing gloves, was really the harbinger of a 21st-century novelty: YouTube.

For Edison, the invention of movies was a diversion from his main interest at the time: extracting iron ore from depleted mines, an obsession that would cost him much of his fortune. If that scheme had not so occupied him, he might not have left the bulk of the film experiment work to his assistant, William Kennedy Laurie Dickson.

That proved to be the cinema's good fortune, for Dickson was a scientist with a gift for the theatrical. (The invaluable Kino DVD *Edison: The Invention of Movies* includes dozens of Dickson's early films.) It was probably he who designed Edison's film studio in West Orange, N.J. Known as the Black Maria, it was a shack that revolved to catch the sun through a skylight. The world's first film director, Dickson also invested his experiments with odd touches that, seen today, look like infant epiphanies.

In *Blacksmith Scene,* which on May 9, 1893, became the first kinetoscope production to be shown publicly, Dickson presents three men wrapped in smithy aprons, their sleeves rolled up, rhythmically pounding an anvil with hammers. These first film actors (Edison Co. employees) pause to take swigs from a beer bottle, then return to work. Initially, the man on the left is partly obscured by a figure facing the action; he realizes he's in the way and ducks out of frame

Left to right, in the first screen kiss, May Irwin and John C. Rice reenact a moment from their Broadway hit, *The Widow Jones*; a bandit in *The Great Train Robbery* prepares to fire directly at the camera.

eight seconds into the 26-second film. So the first movie also had the first blooper.

In 1894-95, Dickson attempted a sound film. In the 17 seconds we have, Dickson is seen on the left playing a violin into a cone-shaped recording instrument. And because even a talking picture had to be a moving picture, the director fills the frame's center with two male employees of the Edison Co., who dance clumsily to the music. Dickson often brought extra characters into his little dramas to add attitude and nuance. In the 1894 *Athlete with Wand*, a muscular gent displays his aesthetic athleticism, but your eye is drawn to a spaniel at the right, which gives a bored glance to the performer and turns its head away.

As the great promoter and the gifted tinkerer, Edison and Dickson anticipated a much later pair of bright boys: Edison was, in a way, Steve Jobs to Dickson's Steve Wozniak. The difference is that Edison couldn't see the magic in their new gadget. But then he was, as Charles Musser writes in *The Emergence of Cinema: The American Screen to 1907,* "the businessman's inventor," making products for plutocrats. As such, he naturally emphasized hardware over software—popular music, movie stories, and stars—that he couldn't understand. Exasperated by his mentor's refusal to think big, Dickson left the company in 1895 to work with several of Edison's rivals.

A scene from *The Life of an American Fireman*, filmed by Edison director Edwin S. Porter the year before he made *The Great Train Robbery.*

The challenge of movie exhibition has always been to create a must-see sensation. As the kinetoscope migrated from the West Orange lab to music halls and arcades, Edison films directed by Dickson, William Heise, Alfred Clark, and Edwin S. Porter reveled in sensational sights and effects. The kinetoscope offered more sex and violence than a mass audience had ever seen before. The films ranged from mini-documentaries (firemen at a blazing house) to vaudeville snippets (Annie Oakley shooting at glass balls) and travelogues (Coney Island, Niagara Falls). But the top sellers were R-rated fare. Nubile Annabelle Moore performed a "serpentine" dance, her hair and gown gaudily hand-colored. In the notorious *Fatima's Dance*, the heavy houri whirls and shimmies, and when the shaking of bosom and booty reaches its climax, two censorious rows of fence posts obscure the action.

Edison's assistant William Dickson plays violin while two Edison staffers dance in one of the earliest attempts at a sound film.

Have a taste for blood sports? The Edison directors staged boxing matches and cockfights. Clark's 1895 *The*

Execution of Mary, Queen of Scots, using trick photography to portray the monarch's beheading, might qualify as the first splatter film. Even grimmer, the 1903 *Electrocuting an Elephant* presented exactly what it promised: the spectacle of Topsy, a Coney Island elephant that had killed three men, standing with cables attached to her body, then collapsing as it sizzles with electricity.

In 1896, the Edison Co. released its most popular picture of the decade and one of its first to be viewed on a large screen. A 20-second excerpt from the Broadway play *The Widow Jones,* it featured two middle-aged stage performers, May Irwin and John C. Rice, embracing, silently chatting, and finally smooching. The movie, known as *The Kiss,* stoked a furor because of its intimacy: two figures in medium close-up engaged in a traditionally private moment. Here was the forerunner of every love story, romantic comedy, and, by extension, stag film. "It turned John C. Rice into a kissing star," Musser says on the Kino DVD. "He appeared in vaudeville giving kissing demonstrations." The Edison Co. had thus produced the movies' first celebrity.

And in Porter, Edison found a director with the vision to expand one- and two-minute vignettes into 10-minute melodramas. Porter's 1902 *The Life of an American Fireman* is a full-fledged action-adventure; it shows the rescue of a woman and her child first from inside a burning building and then from the outside, though both actions would have been simultaneous. Even more daring was *The Great Train Robbery* (1903), which Musser properly calls the first blockbuster. The 10-minute movie comprises 10 urgent tableaux, including the takeover of the train, the assaulting and reviving of a telegraph operator, and the bad guys' escape. It ends with the famous medium close-up of an outlaw aiming his gun straight at the audience and firing away—the money shot seen round the world.

In *Electrocuting an Elephant,* Topsy is executed with alternating current, which Edison long tried to discredit as lethal.

For the next decade, Edison ran the largest studio, but his closest involvement with movies was as head of the Motion Picture Patents Co. (MPPC), a cartel of the main American film producers, most of them based in New York City. The MPPC insisted that films be rented to exhibitors rather than sold outright, forbade its signatories to make feature-length films, and tried to drive independent producers out of business. Edison's rivals were forced to move elsewhere.

In 1917, the MPPC was found guilty of antitrust violations and dissolved; one year later, Edison sold off his Bronx studio and left the film business. But the Wizard's myopic machinations had inadvertently created another industry. By exiling his rivals to Southern California, Edison invented Hollywood.

Richard Corliss is a film critic for TIME magazine.

CEASELESS INVENTION

CHAPTER SIX

Thomas Edison is so well remembered for his work with electricity, the phonograph, and the movie camera, that we forget sometimes how many other inventions and new processes poured forth from his laboratories. Although he closely supervised his phonograph and recording interests until the late 1920s, he washed his hands of the electrical business after the forced merger of his company with Thomson-Houston in 1892, and never paid more than cursory attention to his film-related businesses. Ore extraction, cement production, an electric car—at various times in the last half of his life, he was more absorbed in these than he was in the pursuits his enduring fame rests upon.

By the time he exited the electrical business, Edison's real passion was attempting to revolutionize the business of extracting low-grade iron ore. After the humiliation of the forcible merger, extracting ore was the "big thing" that he had promised his secretary,

Edison at work in his West Orange laboratory.

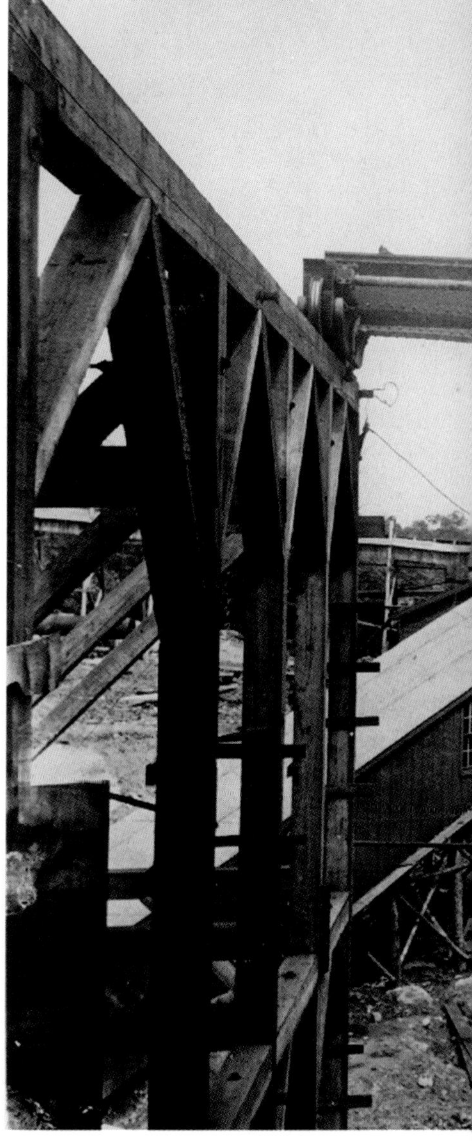

Alfred Tate, he would do to make people forget he had ever been involved with electricity. In the late 1870s, Edison had experimented with techniques to separate gold from crushed rock. By 1882, when he was purchasing large quantities of iron ore to make his first dynamos, he began to think about ways to extract usable iron from the mineral deposits of magnetite that formed long stretches of black sand along the north shore of Long Island, N.Y., formations he had noticed on a fishing trip.

As a first step he built a small experimental plant near the beach and equipped it with an electromagnetic separating device he had designed for his gold-milling pursuits. Sand or crushed rock was poured through a hopper to fall in broad sheets past a line of large magnets that captured any particles of iron and diverted them into bins. The Long Island experiments went well enough for him to establish a commercial operation in Rhode Island that same year, with the aim of selling processed ore to iron and steel mills in the Eastern states. But potential customers found the small-particle iron hard to use, and Edison shut down the Rhode Island plant just months after opening it.

Five years later, in 1887, he returned to the problem. This time, he would go at it in a big way. He established a pilot plant at a mine in Humboldt, Mich., and then another one in Bechtelsville, Pa. He also began to assemble a vast tract of land—which would grow to 19,000 acres—near the town of Ogdensburg in northwestern New Jersey along the Pennsylvania border, an area he had identified as rich in magnetite. There he established a vast quarrying and milling operation, at first employing 145 men, a number that would grow to 400. They lived on the site in a company town, with 50 or so frame houses and a company store.

The milling operation delighted Edison and absorbed much of his time. It also ate up a good deal of his personal fortune. Three years before the forced merger of Edison General Electric, he had realized $3.5 million by cashing out most of his financial stake in the company. Over time, much of that money went to keeping the enormously expensive ore separation scheme running. Mining and milling required costly equipment, like the largest steam shovel in America, to gouge out the giant quarries. "We are making a Yosemite of our own here," he bragged to a reporter in 1892. "We will soon have one of the biggest artificial canyons in the world." Then there were the huge 100-horsepower grinders that smashed the broken rock to smaller pieces and another set of grinders to reduce them to the powder that was sprinkled past the magnets.

Although conditions were primitive, Edison relished life at his mill town and often spent the entire workweek there, returning home exhausted on weekends. He loved the strenuous work and the camaraderie that had a flavor of the old days at his lab at Menlo Park. But business did not go well. There were technical problems with the rock crushing and refining process, and the ore it produced was of poor quality. In 1893, another financial panic gripped the American economy and

A giant crane was part of the operation at Edison's Ogdensburg ore mill.

sent it into a prolonged depression. Then John D. Rockefeller made arrangements to quarry and transport vast amounts of high-quality iron ore from the Mesabi Range in Minnesota, a development that drove down the price of the very ore Edison was trying to sell. He threw in the towel. In 1899, after a decade of losses, he closed the Ogdensburg mill. A few years later, he asked a friend to calculate how much his General Electric stock would be worth if he hadn't sold it to finance the ore operation. The answer was, more than $4 million. Edison paused, then said with a smile, "Well, it's all gone, but we had a hell of a good time spending it!"

Anyway, by that time he was on to other projects. Edison's experience with pulverizing rocks had led him to an interest in the production of cement—the sand produced by his-ore refining process had also been sold, some of it to cement companies. In 1899, soon after closing Ogdensburg, he formed his own cement company with money from a group of investors. Not content, of course, with existing technologies, Edison insisted on designing and testing a new kind of kiln—at

150 feet more than twice the size of standard ones—for roasting the mixture of ground rock and limestone that produces cement.

In 1903, with his New Jersey cement plant still not working at full capacity, he suffered a terrible setback when an explosion and fire killed eight workers, including his chief engineer, causing him to close the plant for redesign. Although he eventually arrived at a satisfactory new kiln, one that would be widely adopted throughout the industry, and his company became one of the largest U.S. producers of cement, the business was often a money loser. To create new demand for his product, in 1906 Edison announced an ingenious idea: low-cost three-story houses for working people. They would be made of concrete poured into giant cast iron sectional molds faced with nickel or brass—as many as 500 for each house. Everything—ceilings, floors, doors, windows, and stairways, even the bathtub—would be cast in one piece. Concrete houses would be fireproof and easy to clean, he promised. They could sell for around $1,200, a third the price of the typical house at that time. And although they would be mass-produced, they wouldn't have to feel stark and featureless. Architects could design decorative detailing into the molds.

Edison's concrete house was another of his ideas that went nowhere. Developers weren't interested, in part because substantial upfront investments were required for the metal molds. A few of the houses were built near West Orange, however, and they still stand. For a time he even tried to promote the idea of concrete home furnishings—phonograph cabinets, bedroom sets, even a piano—made of what he shrewdly called "foam concrete." It didn't fly.

No matter, there were other worlds to conquer. In 1895, the first practical gas-powered automobiles appeared. Four years later, Edison started work on a storage battery, which he hoped could be used to power an electric car. He experimented with a variety of metals for the electrodes before arriving in 1901 at one using nickel and iron, when most competitors used lead. By then, he had also come up with a prototype electric car that could go as fast as 70 miles per hour, one that he later claimed could travel 85 miles without a recharge. Battery production would not begin for two years, time that Edison put to use by talking up his latest invention in the press and conducting highly publicized road tests in electric cars.

Edison with a model of one of his three-story poured-concrete houses. Although Edison hoped they might provide a low-cost housing option for working families, few were ever built.

When it was finally ready for the market, Edison's alkaline, nickel, and iron battery did not at first perform as well as promised. It leaked and lost capacity after just a few recharges. He managed to hold on to business customers, such as retailers, that purchased fleets of battery-powered delivery trucks. But by the time Edison was able to offer a new battery that worked more effectively, in 1910,

Edison, with his son Tom Jr. at the steering bar, prepare to go for a drive in an electric automobile. Though the battery developed by Edison to power cars did not at first work well in them, it proved to have other uses.

gas-powered cars were the preferred vehicles for most drivers. The electric car would be marginalized until it re-emerged a century later as an environmentally conscious alternative to cars that burn fossil fuel. Edison eventually found new markets for his battery, including ships and railways—enough new markets that the battery would turn out to be a very profitable invention for him, if not in the way he had anticipated.

But as an unexpected dividend, Edison's interest in the future of automobiles led him into one of the closest friendships of his adult life. Edison first met Henry Ford in 1896, when Ford, who was 16 years younger, was chief engineer at Edison's bulb-manufacturing plant in Detroit. It was a brief encounter that Edison claimed not even to remember later. The star-struck Ford, however, who had just built a primitive gas-powered car, considered it a turning point in his life. A few words of encouragement from Edison, he said later, convinced him to pursue his work on horseless carriages.

Their next meeting would not come until 1912. By that time, Ford was the famous inventor of the Model T, the low-price gas-powered car that had sealed the fate of electric automobiles. Edison was the head of a struggling battery company whose sales manager, understanding Ford's power in the auto world, had invited him to meet with Edison. Ford came to Edison's lab in West Orange with a proposal—would Edison design an electrical system to start the engines in his cars? Edison came back later with a different idea. Would Ford subsidize Edison's work on the battery? Ford

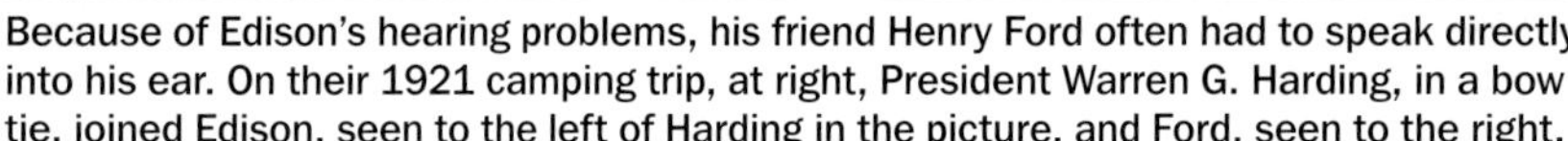

Because of Edison's hearing problems, his friend Henry Ford often had to speak directly into his ear. On their 1921 camping trip, at right, President Warren G. Harding, in a bow tie, joined Edison, seen to the left of Harding in the picture, and Ford, seen to the right.

was only too happy to be assisting his hero. By the end of 1913, Edison had borrowed $700,000 from Ford at 5% interest against future royalties from Edison's batteries. The next year, Ford even announced his intention to begin production of an electric car with an Edison battery.

Late in 1914, Edison would be especially glad of Ford's friendship and money. On the evening of Dec. 9, a fire broke out in a wooden building in his West Orange lab and factory complex where highly inflammable movie film was stored. Soon the fire spread to larger buildings in the compound. Although these were concrete and presumed to be fireproof, they contained materials, used to manufacture phonograph records, that exploded into flames. One Edison worker was killed when he went into a burning building where he mistakenly thought some people might be trapped. Before it was over, fire companies from eight towns had arrived and a crowd of 10,000 to 15,000 gathered to watch.

The 67-year-old Edison was having dinner at home when the fire started. Summoned to the site, he watched impassively as a substantial part of his personal kingdom collapsed in flames. Then he said to his son Charles, who worked at his father's phonograph factory: "Where's Mother? Get her over here, and her friends too. They'll never see a fire like this again."

When it was all over, the main laboratory building and Edison's library had been spared, but 13

of the 18 buildings in the complex were burned out. Because he had expected them to be fireproof, Edison had insured them for only a fraction of their value. But he set to work immediately to secure bank loans to rebuild, and Ford traveled from Michigan to New Jersey to personally present him with a $750,000 loan.

Eventually, Ford built a winter vacation home for himself and his family next to the Edisons' retreat in Fort Myers, Fla. He gave numerous Ford cars to Edison and Mina and even their children. For six years starting in 1918, Edison and Ford went on annual camping trips by car with the tire manufacturer Harvey Firestone. Three of the trips included John Burroughs, a naturalist. They weren't exactly roughing it—a chef, photographer, and caravan of trucks filled with fine food and creature comforts followed them everywhere. One year, their party was joined by President Warren Harding. For his part, Edison was comfortable with Ford because they were on an equal footing as successful businessmen, though Ford was much wealthier. (Unfortunately, Edison also shared some of Ford's notorious anti-Semitic prejudices, though not as fervently or as vocally.) And Ford simply worshipped Edison. In the late 1920s, he even created a shrine to him, a meticulous reconstruction of the Menlo Park lab—complete with soil shipped in from the site—in Greenfield Village, the reconstructed town and complex of museums and attractions that Ford built in Dearborn, Mich.

In 1911, Edison organized most of his remaining businesses into a single company, Thomas A. Edison Inc. He spent his final decades being lionized in the press and in public opinion as a folk hero, America's homespun genius, the father of the modern world. His annual birthday interviews in newspapers became an institution, an opportunity for him to hold forth on all kinds of subjects, from religion (he was a skeptic who could say, "a personal God means absolutely nothing to me"), to diet (Americans "should diminish their intake of food"), to the gold standard (he was against it). And although he had misgivings about America's entry into World War I in 1917, two years earlier he had agreed to serve as head of a board of scientists and industrialists advising the U.S. Navy. It took few of his suggestions, but during wartime he performed many experiments with antisubmarine devices for the government in a lab established for that purpose in West Orange. This effort also was to no avail.

By the 1920s, Edison's children were grown. His oldest, Marion, who had chafed under the rule of her stepmother, Mina, spent years in Europe, survived a disfiguring bout of smallpox, and married and divorced a German military officer before returning home after the war. William Leslie, the younger son from his first marriage, settled into the life of a gentleman farmer. But the older boy, Tom Jr., led a star-crossed life. Having tried and failed to become an inventor, he fell in with fraudsters who got him to lend the Edison name to bogus products like a quack medical device called the "Magno-Electric Vitalizer." In 1903, his father arrived at a legal agreement with his son barring him from using the family name in business ventures. Although he reconciled with his father, and even went to work for his company, after years of heavy drinking, Tom Jr. died in 1935.

Of his children by Mina, Madeleine went to Bryn Mawr and then married. Their unscientific but business-minded middle child, Charles, was his father's chosen successor. Named as Edison's "first assistant" in 1914, when he was 24, he would take over the Edison company after his father's retirement 12 years later. He was briefly Secretary of the Navy under Franklin Roosevelt and then became governor of New Jersey in 1941. Their younger boy, Theodore, studied engineering and physics at M.I.T., became an inventor himself, and lived in West Orange until he died in 1992, the last of Edison's surviving children. Because none of Edison's sons had children, the family name died with him.

In the 1920s, Edison's phonograph business began to falter, partly because of an economic downturn and the pressure of a new competitor: radio. People no longer needed to buy recordings to listen to music at home. It was available for free over the airwaves to anyone who owned a receiver. Edison's sons Charles and Theodore understood that radio was the future of home entertainment. Their father didn't want to hear it. They urged him to let the company produce a phonograph-radio combination, but Edison was convinced that broadcast sound had so much distortion he didn't want his name associated with what he insisted was the "radio fad."

In 1927, Edison embarked on one of his final explorations, to find a domestic plant substitute for natural rubber. The rise of the automobile had increased demand for rubber. With money from Ford and Firestone he set up an experimental farm on nine acres near his winter home in Fort Myers, Fla., and threw himself into the project with relish. "Everything turned to rubber in the family," his wife later recalled. "We talked rubber, thought rubber, dreamed rubber." But the effort floundered. Meanwhile, his sons finally got his permission to begin making radios and radio-phono combinations, but only as high-end merchandise in deluxe cabinets. These expensive products came on the market just as the Great Depression was getting under way. Barely a year after they began selling them, or trying to, the Edison company ceased production. It had stopped

For the 50th anniversary of the phonograph, Edison recreates his first recording of "Mary Had a Little Lamb."

manufacturing records the year before. As with electricity and filmmaking, the other industries he set in motion, Edison was now out of the music business.

There was a larger problem for Edison than his resistance to consumer taste. As his biographer Paul Israel puts it in *Edison: A Life of Invention*: "By the 1920s, the increase in scientific and technical knowledge had begun to make a generalist such as Edison increasingly outmoded." He had once put together a team of clock makers and machinists adaptable to any task. Now he lacked the more specialized and university-trained chemists to seriously investigate arcane questions of metallurgy or the synthetics that would turn out to be the solution to the rubber shortage during World War II. He wasn't prepared for the realms the 20th century was advancing into, theoretical fields that would all the same spawn new technologies and consumer products. He had created the first model of the modern world of research and development, but a more sophisticated model was now overtaking his.

In any case, his health was declining. In October 1929, for the 50th anniversary of Edison's invention of his incandescent bulb, Ford arranged for a massive celebration at Greenfield Village. The 500 guests to "Light's Golden Jubilee" included John D. Rockefeller Jr., the airplane co-inventor Orville Wright, the scientist Marie Curie, and President Herbert Hoover. The culmination required Edison to perform a dramatic reenactment of his lighting the first incandescent bulb, all of it carried live on radio. He played his part, but the effort caused him to collapse and require bed rest at Ford's home for several days.

In these last years, Edison lived on almost nothing but several glasses of milk a day. When he worked, it was usually at home. The final crisis started in the summer of 1931, when Edison's kidneys began to fail. There followed months of increasing weakness. On October 18, he died at home with his family gathered round. He was 84.

Edison's death became a time of national mourning. His coffin sat for two days in the library of his West Orange lab, with longtime employees forming an honor guard. On the first day, 10,000 people paid their respects. On the next day, 40,000. But there would be a much larger tribute. Taking up a suggestion first made by the governor of New Jersey, President Hoover asked all Americans to turn off their electric lights at 10 p.m. Eastern time on the night of Edison's funeral. Many complied. The broadcast networks also observed a minute of silence. In homes and businesses, the world for a moment went dark. But to make it bright again, people had only to reach for the switch that Thomas Edison had put in their hands.

CREDITS

A window display for the light bulb's Oct. 1879 birthday. Mazda bulbs were a General Electric product line.

FRONT COVER
Photo-illustration by Arthur Hochstein, Edison: Photo Researchers/Getty Images; Bulb: High Impact Photography/Getty Images

BACK COVER
Bettmann/Corbis

TITLE PAGE
Superstock Inc./Getty Images

MASTHEAD PAGES
Corbis

CONTENTS PAGES
Division of Work & Industry, National Museum of American History/Smithsonian Institution

INTRODUCTION
6 (left) Bettmann/Corbis; David Caudery/MacFormat Magazine via Getty Images **7** (clockwise from top) Bettmann/Corbis; Gavin Hellier/JAI/Corbis; Science and Society Picture Library/Getty Images **8** (left) Museum of American Finance; Jean Miele/Corbis **9** (left) Science and Society Picture Library/Getty Images; Alex Potemkin/Getty Images

CHAPTER ONE
11 Bettmann/Corbis **13** (clockwise from top left) Topham/The Image Works, Thomas Edison National Historic Park; Corbis **15** (top) Mary Evans/Everett Collection; AP Images **16** Church Archives, The Church of Jesus Christ of Latter-day Saints. Salt Lake City **17** (left) Con Tanasiuk/Design Pics/Corbis; The Granger Collection

CHAPTER TWO
19 Bettmann/Corbis **21** (top) DeA Picture Library/The Granger Collection; H. Zimmer **22** Thomas Edison National Historic Park **23** Topham/The Image Works (2) **24** Michael Freeman/Corbis **25** Bridgeman Art Library **26** Universal Images Group via Getty Images **27** Apic/Getty Images

MENLO PARK
29 AISA/Everett Collection **30** (from top) The Granger Collection; Division of Work & Industry, National Museum of American History/Smithsonian Institution; Mondadori via Getty Images **31** (clockwise form top) Keystone/Getty Images; Underwood & Underwood/Corbis; Division of Work & Industry, National Museum of American History/Smithsonian Institution

CHAPTER THREE
33 Matthew Brady/Library of Congress Prints & Photographs Division **34** (top) Science and Society Picture Library/The Image Works; no credit **35** Graphic by Andrea Ford; Illustration by John Burgoyne for TIME **37** (left to right) Thomas Edison National Historic Park; Corbis; Thomas Edison National Historic Park **38** Science and Society Picture Library/Getty Images **40** Thomas Edison National Historic Park **41** Thomas Edison National Historic Park (3)
42 (clockwise from top left) Science and Society Picture Library/The Image Works (2); Science and Society Picture Library/Science Museum/Art Resource, NY; Science and Society Picture Library/Getty Images **43** (clockwise from top left) Mary Evans/Science Source; Science and Society Picture Library/Getty Images; Blank Archives/Getty Images; Science and Society Picture Library/The Image Works **44** Thomas Edison National Historic Park **46** Thomas Edison National Historic Park **48** Bettmann/Corbis **49** (clockwise from top left) Science and Society Picture Library/Getty Images; Stock Montage/Getty Images; Collection of René Rondeau

CHAPTER FOUR
51 Photo-illustration by Arthur Hochstein, Bulb Photo by High Impact Photography/Getty Images **52** The Granger Collection **53** Jerry McCrea/Star Ledger/Corbis **55** Graphic by Andrea Ford; Illustration by John Burgoyne for TIME **56** Barbara Cushing/Everett Collection **58** Thomas Edison National Historic Park (4) **59** Universal Images Group via Getty Images **60** New York Public Library/Photo Researchers/Getty Images **61** Jerry McCrea/Star Ledger/Corbis

ELECTRIFYING AMERICA
62 Hulton Archive/Getty Images **63** (top) Bettmann/Corbis; Photo Researchers/Getty Images **64** Bettmann/Corbis **65** Sheila Terry/Science Source **66** Schenectady Museum, Hall of Electrical History Foundation/Corbis

THE ELECTRIC CHAIR
69 The Granger Collection

BRIGHT LIGHTS, BIG CITIES
70 Hulton Archive/Getty Images **72** Corbis **73** (clockwise from top) Bettmann/Corbis; PEMCO, Webster & Stevens Collection, Museum of History and Industry, Seattle/Corbis; William Henry Jackson, Field Museum Library/Getty Images

CHAPTER FIVE
75 Thomas Edison National Historic Park **76** Corbis **78** The Granger Collection **79** Graphic by Andrea Ford; Illustration by John Burgoyne for TIME **80** Thomas Edison National Historic Park **81** (top) Thomas Edison National Historic Park; Science and Society Picture Library/Getty Images

THE MOVIES ARE BORN
82 (top) Library of Congress Prints and Photographs Division; John Kobal Foundation/Getty Images **83** John Springer Collection/Corbis **84** (top) no credit; Thomas Edison National Historic Park **85** no credit

CHAPTER SIX
87 Library of Congress/Science Faction/Corbis **89** Thomas Edison National Historic Park **90** Corbis **91** Bettmann/Corbis **92** Bettmann/Corbis **93** Corbis **95** Hulton-Deutsch Collection/Corbis

THIS PAGE
96 Schenectady Museum, Hall of Electrical History Foundation/Corbis-